Quick & Easy
Celebration Cakes

Quick & Easy
Celebration Cakes

Joanna Farrow

First published in Great Britain in 2004 by
Hamlyn, a division of Octopus Publishing Group Ltd
This edition published in 2006 by Bounty Books, a
division of Octopus Publishing Group Ltd
2–4 Heron Quays, London E14 4JP

Reprinted 2006, 2007

ISBN 13: 978-0-753713-69-3
ISBN 10: 0-753713-69-1

A CIP catalogue record for this book is available
from the British Library.
Printed and bound in China

NOTES
Standard level spoon measures
are used in all recipes.
1 tablespoon = one 15 ml spoon
1 teaspoon = one 5 ml spoon

Both metric and imperial measurements are
given for the recipes. Use one set of
measures only, not a mixture of both.

Ovens should be preheated to the specified
temperature. If using a fan assisted oven,
follow the manufacturer's instructions for
adjusting the time and temperature.

Medium eggs have been used throughout.

Contents

Introduction 6

Equipment 8

Cake recipes 10

Icings and fillings 16

Techniques 20

Finishing touches 24

Something for everyone 26

Hearts and flowers 60

Seasonal treats 84

Party time 112

Index 142

Acknowledgements 144

Introduction

No one ever quite grows out of the thrill of being presented with a fabulous cake, whether it's for a birthday, to acknowledge a special achievement or to mark an anniversary or, perhaps even, a wedding day. The theme and occasion might change, but from the simplest buttercream-covered cake to a spectacular tiered creation, the cake usually takes centre stage at any party, and its cutting is the moment when everyone comes together and toasts the special guest or couple.

Unfortunately, as most of us know only too well, celebrations and parties can be expensive affairs, and having a cake made professionally can be one expense too far. This book aims to show just how easy it is to make and decorate a cake that is the equal of anything you might buy. All the cakes use basic equipment and ingredients that are available from most supermarkets and high-street stores. You'll probably have some of the baking tins in your kitchen already, and even if you don't, all the cakes used in this book are regular sizes, so you'll have no difficulty in finding suitable baking tins in your local kitchenware or department store. You can also hire, surprisingly inexpensively, some extra large or unusually shaped tins from specialist cake-decorating stores. Many of the larger stores offer a mail-order service, so even if you don't have a store near to you, it's possible that they will be able to supply the items you need.

The first section of the book contains some basic recipes for the cakes themselves. Don't be put off if you've never made a cake before. There's a buttery Madeira cake, a moist rich fruit cake and a simply mouth-watering chocolate cake that are well within the grasp of the first-time baker. Of course, if you simply can't face making the cake, look in your local supermarkets for ready-made sponges and fruit cakes. Some of them are perfectly acceptable in flavour, although they tend to be rather small and shallow. You can certainly use these for the smaller cakes in the book, stacking round ones together to create depth or lining up rectangular loaf cakes to make a larger square. Use a little buttercream, jam or a strip of almond paste to secure them together and no one will know the difference! For wedding cakes and cakes for special gatherings try a local baker or delicatessen, which sometimes supply larger fruit and sponge cakes. And don't forget that you can perk up a bought cake by drizzling it with a little liqueur before covering it with icing.

The time taken to decorate the cakes shown in this book ranges from about 20 minutes for the simplest designs to a couple of hours for the more elaborate creations, such as the White Chocolate Wedding Cake on page 66. You can prepare many of the individual elements of decorations, such as chocolate curls, well in advance, and, of course, the cakes themselves can be made when you have some spare time and frozen until they are needed.

Seasonal and family celebration cakes play a large part in this book. Involve your family in helping you make these cakes – they'll get as much fun from decorating them as they will from eating them.

Equipment

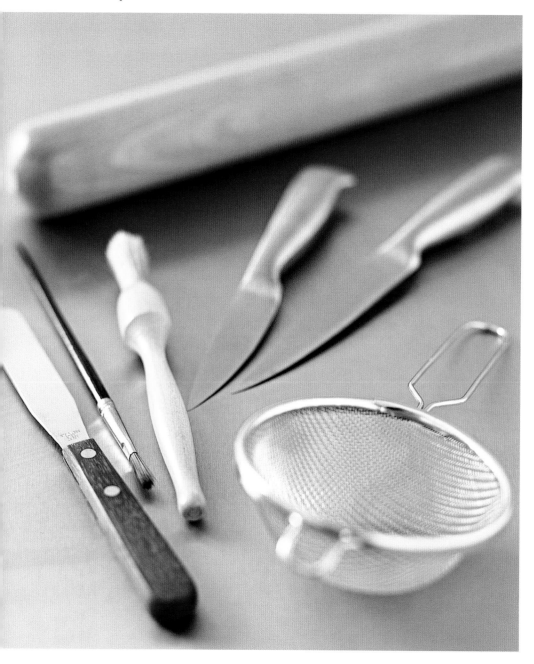

The recipes in this book are generally quick and easy to make and to assemble, so the amount of equipment you will need is minimal. Most of the items required are ones that you'll probably have already, such as a rolling pin, palette knives, sieves, sharp knives, scissors and some artist's paintbrushes. If there's a piece of equipment you need to buy, it's well worth visiting your local cake-decorating store. These are usually packed with cutters, tools, ready-made decorations, coloured icings and almost every food colouring imaginable. If you don't have a local store, many of the larger kitchenware companies offer a useful mail order service.

BASIC EQUIPMENT

- kitchen scales
- rolling pin
- large and small knives
- large and small palette knives
- pastry brush
- artist's paintbrushes
- scissors
- selection of bowls in various sizes
- small sieve or tea strainer
- baking tins
- greaseproof and baking parchment
- whisk

CAKE TINS

If you decide to make your own cakes – a Madeira sponge, a chocolate cake or a fruit cake – it's worth investing in good, strong cake tins, which will last for years. A round tin, 20 cm (8 inches) across, or a square one, 18 cm (7 inches), is a particularly useful size. Choose a tin that is about 7.5 cm (3 inches) deep. A loose base makes it easier to remove the cake but is not essential. Other useful tins include a 12-section muffin tin (perfect for cupcakes), a 33 x 23 cm (13 x 9 inch) shallow baking tin for Swiss rolls, and a couple of sturdy baking sheets for cooking meringues or setting out delicate piped decorations.

   Before you bake a cake in a deep cake tin, you need to line both the base and sides of the tin with greaseproof paper. Melt a little butter or margarine and brush it over the base and sides of the tin first so that the paper sticks in position.

LINING A ROUND TIN

Using the tin as a guide, draw a circle on the greaseproof paper and cut it out. Cut strips of paper a little wider than the height of the tin, fold over a lip about 1 cm (½ inch) wide and snip it at intervals. Fit the paper around the sides of the tin so the lip sits flat on the base. If you need more than one strip of paper to go round the sides, overlap them slightly. Press the circle into the base and brush all the paper with more melted butter or margarine.

LINING A SQUARE TIN

This technique is similar to the one above, but once you've cut the square base and strips, you only need to make snips in the paper at the corners to make sure it fits squarely into the corners of the tin. Brush the paper with a little more melted butter or margarine.

Cake recipes

For most of the recipes in this book you can choose between using bought or homemade cakes. Although bought cakes are convenient, they tend to be quite small and shallow. Some supermarkets sell rich fruit and Madeira 'ready-to-decorate' celebration cakes, but these sometimes have piped icing decorations, which limit the scope for the additional decorations you might have in mind.

If you have the time, make your own. You have an unlimited choice of size, it's cheaper and, of course, it will taste better. All the cakes in this section are incredibly easy to make, even if you've no previous experience of cake making. They can all be made well ahead and frozen for several weeks, or, in the case of the Rich Fruit Cake, wrapped well and stored in a cool place for several months.

MADEIRA CAKE

SQUARE CAKE	12 cm (5 inch)	15 cm (6 inch)	18 cm (7 inch)	20 cm (8 inch)	23 cm (9 inch)
ROUND CAKE	15 cm (6 inch)	18 cm (7 inch)	20 cm (8 inch)	23 cm (9 inch)	25 cm (10 inch)
Serves	8	12	16	20	24
Cooking time	40 minutes	50–60 minutes	1 hour	1–1¼ hours	1¼–1½ hours
Unsalted butter, softened	175 g (6 oz)	225 g (7½ oz)	300 g (10 oz)	375 g (12 oz)	475 g (15 oz)
Caster sugar	175 g (6 oz)	225 g (7½ oz)	300 g (10 oz)	375 g (12 oz)	475 g (15 oz)
Medium eggs	3	4	5	6	8
Milk	2 tablespoons	3 tablespoons	4 tablespoons	5 tablespoons	150 ml (¼ pint)
Self-raising flour	250 g (8 oz)	300 g (10 oz)	400 g (13 oz)	625 g (1¼ lb)	750 g (1½ lb)
FLAVOUR VARIATIONS					
Vanilla					
Vanilla extract	1 teaspoon	2 teaspoons	1 tablespoon	4 teaspoons	2 tablespoons
Orange or lemon	(substitute juice for milk)				
Orange or lemon zest	zest of 1	zest of 1	zest of 1½	zest of 2	zest of 3
Orange or lemon juice	2 tablespoons	3 tablespoons	4 tablespoons	5 tablespoons	150 ml (¼ pint)
Chocolate	(substitute cocoa powder for equal amount of flour)				
Cocoa powder	25 g (1 oz)	40 g (1½ oz)	50 g (2 oz)	65 g (2½ oz)	75 g (3 oz)

1 Using a wooden spoon or electric whisk, cream the butter and sugar together until light and fluffy. Lightly beat the eggs with the milk in a separate bowl. Gradually beat the eggs and milk into the creamed mixture, alternating with the flour.

2 Turn the mixture into the prepared tin and level the surface. Bake in a preheated oven, 160°C (325°F), Gas Mark 3, for the time indicated in the chart or until a skewer, inserted in the centre, comes out cleanly. Leave the cake in the tin for 10 minutes, then transfer it to a wire rack to cool.

SWISS ROLL

1 Grease and line a Swiss roll tin, 33 x 23 cm (13 x 9 inch). Put the eggs and sugar in a large, heatproof bowl over a pan of gently simmering water and whisk until the mixture is light and airy and the whisk leaves a trail when lifted from the bowl. Remove from the heat and whisk for a further 3 minutes.

2 Sift the flour over the bowl and use a large metal spoon to fold it in, adding 1 tablespoon hot water once most of the flour is incorporated. Turn into the tin and gently spread the mixture into the corners. Bake in a preheated oven, 200°C (400°F), Gas Mark 6 for 10–12 minutes until pale golden and just firm to the touch.

3 While the cake is baking, sprinkle a sheet of greaseproof paper with caster sugar. Turn the warm cake out on to the paper and spread it with the jam. Starting from a short end, roll up the sponge. Place it seam-side down on a wire rack to cool.

Serves 10

3 large eggs

100 g (3½ oz) caster sugar

100 g (3½ oz) plain flour

extra caster sugar, for dusting

6–8 tablespoons raspberry or strawberry jam

VANILLA CUPCAKES

Makes 12

150 g (5 oz) unsalted butter, softened

150 g (5 oz) caster sugar

175 g (6 oz) self-raising flour

3 eggs

2 teaspoons vanilla extract

1 Line a 12-section muffin tray with paper cake cases. Put all the ingredients in a bowl and beat with a hand-held electric whisk for 1–2 minutes until the mixture is light and creamy. Divide the mixture among the cases.

2 Bake in a preheated oven, 180°C (350°F), Gas Mark 4, for 18–20 minutes until they are risen and just firm to the touch. Transfer the cakes to a wire rack to cool.

Paper cake cases come in various sizes. For the recipes in this book it's best to use muffin cases, which are slightly larger than the cases sold for making fairy cakes.

RICH CHOCOLATE CAKE

SQUARE CAKE	12 cm (5 inch)	18 cm (7 inch)	23 cm (9 inch)
ROUND CAKE	15 cm (6 inch)	20 cm (8 inch)	25 cm (10 inch)
Serves	10	18	24
Cooking time	1 hour	1¼ hours	1½ hours
Cocoa powder	75 g (3 oz)	125 g (4oz)	175 g (6 oz)
Boiling water	250 ml (8 fl oz)	375 ml (13 fl oz)	575 ml (18 fl oz)
Unsalted butter, softened	125 g (4 oz)	200 g (7 oz)	325 g (11 oz)
Light muscovado sugar	275 g (9 oz)	400 g (14 oz)	700 g (1½ lb)
Plain flour	200 g (7 oz)	300 g (10 oz)	500 g (1 lb)
Baking powder	1 teaspoon	1½ teaspoons	2½ teaspoons
Eggs, beaten	2	3	5

1 Put the cocoa powder in a bowl and gradually whisk in the boiling water until smooth. Leave to cool.

2 Beat together the butter and sugar until they are creamy. Gradually beat in the eggs, a little at a time, adding a little of the flour to prevent curdling. Sift the remaining flour over the bowl with the baking powder. Use a large metal spoon to fold in the flour. Stir in the cocoa mixture.

3 Turn the mixture into the prepared tin. Bake in a preheated oven, 180°C (350°F), Gas Mark 4, for the time stated in the chart or until the crust is just firm. For a good, moist texture the centre of the cake should have a very slight wobble when it comes out of the oven.

4 Leave to cool in the tin, then wrap and store for up to 3 days in a cool place or freeze.

RICH FRUIT CAKE

SQUARE CAKE	12 cm (5 inch)	18 cm (7 inch)	23 cm (9 inch)
ROUND CAKE	15 cm (6 inch)	20 cm (8 inch)	25 cm (10 inch)
Serves	14	24	40
Cooking time	2–2½ hours	3½–3¾ hours	4–4½ hours
Unsalted butter, softened	150 g (5 oz)	250 g (8 oz)	425 g (14 oz)
Light muscovado sugar	150 g (5 oz)	250 g (8 oz)	425 g (14 oz)
Eggs, beaten	3	5	8
Plain flour	200 g (7 oz)	325 g (11 oz)	625 g (1¼ lb)
Ground mixed spice	2 teaspoons	1 tablespoon	2 tablespoons
Stem ginger, chopped	25 g (1 oz)	40 g (1½ oz)	65 g (2½ oz)
Luxury mixed dried fruit	625 g (1¼ lb)	1 kg (2 lb)	2 kg (4 lb)
Blanched chopped almonds	50 g (2 oz)	75 g (3 oz)	100 g (3½ oz)

1 Beat together the butter and sugar until creamy. Gradually beat in the eggs, a little at a time, adding a little of the flour if the mixture starts to curdle.

2 Sift the flour with the spice and stir into the mixture. Add the ginger, dried fruit and almonds and stir the ingredients until evenly combined.

3 Turn the mixture into the prepared tin and level the surface. Bake in a preheated oven, 140°C (275°F), Gas Mark 1, for the time indicated in the chart or until a skewer, inserted into the centre, comes out cleanly. Leave to cool in the tin.

4 Remove the cake from the tin and wrap it in foil. If necessary, you can store it for up to 6 months in a cool, dry place until you are ready to ice it.

tip

Once the cake is baked you can drizzle it with brandy, sherry or an orange-flavoured liqueur before storing it. This will enhance the flavour and keep it moist. Pierce the top of the cake all over with a fine skewer and spoon over the liqueur, allowing about 3 tablespoons for a small cake and up to 7–8 tablespoons for a larger one.

CHOUX PASTRY BUNS

Makes 40

125 g (4 oz) plain flour

100 g (3½ oz) unsalted butter, cut
    into pieces

4 eggs, beaten

1 Sift the flour onto a piece of paper. Melt the butter in a medium
saucepan with 300 ml (½ pint) water. Bring to the boil and tip the
flour into the saucepan. Beat with a wooden spoon over the heat
for about 1 minute or until the mixture forms a ball in the centre of
the pan. Leave to cool for 2 minutes.

2 Gradually beat in the eggs, a little at a time, until the paste is
smooth and glossy. Using 2 teaspoons, place spoonfuls of the
paste on baking sheets, spacing them about 5 cm (2 inches) apart.
You should have enough mixture for about 40 small spoonfuls.

3 Bake in a preheated oven, at 220°C (425°F), Gas Mark 7,
for about 20 minutes until the buns are well risen and golden.
Remove from the oven and make a slit in the side of each bun to
allow the steam to escape. Return them to the oven for a further
3–5 minutes until they are firm. Transfer the buns to a wire rack
to cool.

Icings and fillings

Some icings – including buttercream and ganache – are used both as a filling for a cake and as a delicious coating. Others, such as 'ready-to-roll' icing, are used only as a cake covering. Refer to the individual recipes for guidance.

Buttercream can be flavoured (see chart below), but remember that coffee will alter the colour of the buttercream. Bear this in mind if you're using it as a cake covering rather than as a filling.

BUTTERCREAM

Buttercream (or butter icing) has a delicious flavour and excellent texture, and it is extremely versatile. For the best flavour use a good-quality, unsalted butter and beat it thoroughly with the icing sugar so it's easy to apply. Spread the cake with a thin layer of the buttercream first to stick the crumbs in place, which will make a manageable base for the rest of the buttercream. Freshly packed icing sugar is usually fine to use straight from the pack, but if you open it and it looks a bit lumpy, sift it first.

1 Beat the butter and a little of the icing sugar together in a bowl until smooth.

2 Gradually beat in the remaining icing sugar and hot water until pale and creamy.

QUANTITY	single	double	triple	quadruple
Unsalted butter, softened	75 g (3 oz)	150 g (5 oz)	250 g (8 oz)	300 g (10 oz)
Icing sugar	125 g (4 oz)	250 g (8 oz)	375 g (12 oz)	500 g (1 lb)
Hot water	1 teaspoon	2 teaspoons	3 teaspoons	4 teaspoons
FLAVOUR VARIATIONS				
Vanilla extract	½ teaspoon	1 teaspoon	1½ teaspoons	2 teaspoons
Citrus rind (use fruit juice instead of hot water)	2 teaspoons	4 teaspoons	6 teaspoons	8 teaspoons
Coffee granules dissolved in hot water	1 teaspoon in 1 teaspoon water	2 teaspoons in 1 tablespoon water	3 teaspoons in 1 tablespoon water	4 teaspoons in 2 tablespoons water
Cocoa powder dissolved in hot water	1 tablespoon in 1 tablespoon water	2 tablespoons in 2 tablespoons water	3 tablespoons in 3 tablespoons water	4 tablespoons in 4 tablespoons water

GANACHE

Ganache is one of the most luxurious of all the icings, a pure blend of velvety smooth chocolate and cream. Once made, it'll need 15–30 minutes to thicken up before use, but keep an eye on it because it will gradually become too thick to use. This quantity makes enough to cover a 20 cm (8 inch) round cake.

Dark chocolate ganache

300 ml (½ pint) double cream

300 g (10 oz) good quality dark chocolate, chopped

1 Heat the cream in a medium, heavy-based saucepan until it is bubbling around the edge. Remove from the heat and stir in the chopped chocolate.

2 Leave to stand until the chocolate has melted. Turn the mixture into a bowl and chill until the ganache is cool enough to hold its shape. The cooling time will depend on the temperature the cream is heated to. As a guide, check after about 15 minutes, although it might take 30–40 minutes.

White chocolate ganache

300 ml (½ pint) double cream

300 g (10 oz) good quality white chocolate, chopped

1 Heat half the cream in a medium, heavy-based saucepan until it is bubbling around the edges. Remove from the heat and stir in the chocolate.

2 Leave to stand until the chocolate has melted. Turn the mixture into a bowl and chill for about 15 minutes until cold.

3 Stir in the remaining cream and whisk with a hand-held electric whisk until the ganache just holds its shape. Don't over-whisk the mixture or the cream will start to curdle.

CHOCOLATE FUDGE ICING

This icing develops a fudge-like consistency when set, making a delicious filling and covering for chocolate or Madeira cakes. It thickens as it cools, so make sure you use it while it is spreadable. If it does solidify before you've had a chance to use it, simply beat in a dash of hot water. It's an easy recipe to double up on quantities if you've made a larger cake. This quantity makes enough to cover a 15 cm (6 inch) round cake.

25 g (1 oz) unsalted butter

15 g (½ oz) cocoa powder

175 g (6 oz) icing sugar

2 tablespoons milk

1 Melt the butter in a small saucepan. Stir in the cocoa powder and cook, stirring constantly, for 30 seconds until smooth. Remove the pan from the heat and gradually stir in the icing sugar (no need to sift) and milk, mixing until smooth.

2 Return to the heat for 1 minute, stirring constantly until it has a glossy pouring consistency. Quickly spread the icing over the cakes while it is still warm.

ROYAL ICING

Royal icing hardens once it dries out. To compensate for this if you're making a wedding or Christmas cake in advance, beat in a teaspoon of glycerine. If you're not using the icing immediately, press a sheet of clingfilm directly over the surface of the icing to prevent a crust forming. This quantity makes enough to cover a 20 cm (8 inch) round cake.

2 egg whites

500 g (1 lb) icing sugar

1 Use a hand-held electric whisk to beat the egg whites in a large bowl with a little of the icing sugar until smooth.

2 Gradually whisk in the remaining icing sugar until the icing is softly peaking. You might not need all the icing sugar.

Techniques

The techniques for icing and decorating specific cakes accompany the individual recipes, but here are a few basic techniques that crop up frequently throughout the book.

USING READY-TO-ROLL ICING

Soft and pliable, shop-bought, ready-to-roll icing is both easy and fun to use. Large packs of white icing are widely available, and many large supermarkets sell smaller packs of icings in basic colours. For a more interesting range of colours try your local cake-decorating supplier, where you should find a good range of different colours in handy 250 g (8 oz) packs. Once the pack is opened, the icing will gradually dry out, making it impossible to use. To prevent this, tightly wrap any unused icing in clingfilm, even if it's just for a short time. Leftover icing can be stored in a cool place for several months or in the freezer. Before using, knead it with a bit of icing sugar to remove any stickiness.

FOOD COLOURINGS

Food colourings are available in several forms. Liquid colours – the type often available in supermarkets – tend to be less intense, so you might not be able to reach the shade you want before the icing has become too wet. They are useful for pastel shades or for painting on to icing, however.

Paste colours are much more intense and come in a wider range of colours. Basic ones, including red and black, can be bought from supermarkets, but for a much wider choice, visit a specialist cake-decorating store.

Powder colours, also available from cake-decorating stores, can be kneaded into icing. They are more often dusted on to icing, once the icing is shaped and set. Gold and silver food colours are available in liquid form (just give it a stir before use) or as a powder, which can be mixed to a 'paint' with a dash of flavourless cooking oil or a drop of vodka. Check that metallic colours are edible. If they're not, don't apply them directly to the cake, or remove this part of the icing before cutting the cake.

Colouring white icing

Dust your work surface with icing sugar and lightly knead the icing to soften it. Dot the icing with paste colouring using the tip of a cocktail stick. A little paste colour goes a long way, so add it cautiously at first, particularly if you want a pastel shade. You can always add more colour later. If you're adding liquid colour use a cocktail stick or the handle of a teaspoon.

Knead the icing until the colour is evenly distributed. For a marbled effect, leave the icing streaked with colour.

COVERING A CAKE BOARD WITH ICING

Cakes look more 'finished' if you cover the cake board with icing. This can be done either once the cake is iced on the board and only the edges show or, if a lot of the board shows, before the cake is positioned.

To cover the whole board, brush the surface of the board with water. Thinly roll out the icing on a surface dusted with icing sugar and then lift it over the board. Smooth out the icing with the palms of your hands and use a sharp knife to trim off the excess paste around the edges.

To cover the edges of the board, brush the top edge of the board very lightly with water. Roll out long, thin strips of the icing trimmings and lay them around the cake, butting a neat cut edge against the cake. Smooth down and trim off the excess around the edges of the board. For a square cake, it's easiest to cover one side of the board at a time, mitring the icing at the corners. For a round cake, work with the longest strip you can manage, to prevent too many joins.

COVERING WITH READY-TO-ROLL ICING

1 Using a palette knife, spread the top and sides of the cake with a thin layer of smooth apricot or red fruit jam or buttercream.

2 Lightly knead the icing on a surface dusted with icing sugar to soften it slightly and roll it out to a round or square that's about 12 cm (5 inches) larger in diameter than the cake. Lift the icing over a rolling pin and drape it over the cake.

3 Smooth the icing over the top of the cake and ease it to fit around the sides. Because icing is so pliable you should be able to shape it around the sides without leaving any creases.

4 Trim off the excess icing. Using the palms of your hands dusted with icing sugar and a 'dusting' action, smooth out any bumps, making the surface as smooth and flat as you can.

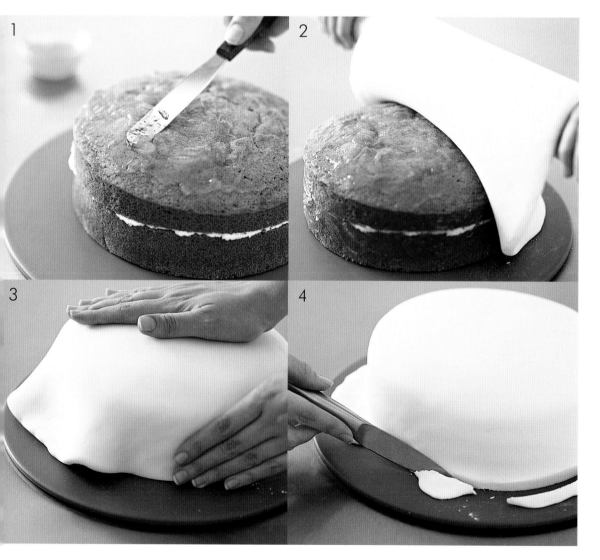

tip

Cake-decorating stores sell icing 'smoothers', which are specially designed to help you get a good, flat surface on the cake. It's worth investing in one if you intend to make several cakes or if you're making one for a special celebration.

COVERING A CAKE WITH ALMOND PASTE

Rich fruit cakes are usually covered with a layer of almond paste before they are iced. Use exactly the same technique as for covering a cake with ready-to-roll icing. Spread the rich fruit cake with apricot jam and then add the almond paste.

There's no need to let the almond paste dry out before covering it with either ready-to-roll or royal icing.

QUANTITIES OF ALMOND PASTE

Square cake	12 cm (5 inch)	18 cm (7 inch)	23 cm (9 inch)
Round cake	15 cm (6 inch)	20 cm (8 inch)	25 cm (10 inch)
Almond paste	400 g (13 oz)	750 g (1½ lb)	1.25 kg (2½ lb)

Finishing touches

The easiest finishing touches can be the most appealing and effective. Adding cut-out shapes or an abundance of fresh flowers will make any cake look extra special.

CUTTING OUT ICING SHAPES

Ready-to-roll icing is ideal for cutting out decorative shapes, ranging from simple stars and hearts to larger designs, such as the theatrical masks on page 58. The shapes can be applied directly to the cake or left on a baking sheet lined with greaseproof paper or baking parchment until they have set hard.

Roll out the icing very thinly on a surface dusted with icing sugar and cut out the shapes. So that the icing doesn't stick, dip the cutter or knife in icing sugar first. Gently transfer the cut-out shapes to the cake or paper.

PIPED ICING

Tubes of icing are readily available from larger stores, but you can make your own paper piping bag if you prefer.

Cut out a square, 25 cm (10 inches), of greaseproof paper or baking parchment and fold the paper diagonally in half to make a triangle. Cut along the folded line. Holding the centre of the long edge towards you, curl the right-hand point of the triangle over to meet the centre point, forming a cone. Bring the left-hand point over the cone so the three points meet. Fold the paper over several times at the points to stop the paper unravelling. Half-fill the bag with your chosen icing and fold up the open end to secure the bag before snipping off the tip. Begin by snipping off a tiny amount to see how finely the mixture flows out. You can easily snip off a bit more for a wider line of piping.

CHOCOLATE CURLS

Curls made by paring chocolate directly from a bar always look good and take very little effort. The chunkier the bar of chocolate, the better the curls will be. Use a vegetable peeler.

MELTING CHOCOLATE

When you're melting chocolate on its own, you need to take a little extra care because it will spoil if you overheat it.

Break the chocolate into pieces and put it in a heatproof bowl. Rest the bowl over a pan of very gently simmering water, but make sure that the base of the bowl does not come into contact with the water. Stir the chocolate occasionally until it has melted, then carefully lift the bowl from the heat. If you're tipping the chocolate out on to a surface such as marble, to make caraque (see page 66), make sure the condensation under the bowl doesn't drip on to the chocolate or it will no longer be workable.

FLOWERS

If you have a stunning array of fresh flowers on a cake, no additional decoration is needed. If the cut ends are out of sight, you can wrap them in a ball of moist cotton wool, secured in clingfilm so that the moisture doesn't spoil the icing.

Realistic-looking artificial flowers, or dried flowers, can also look really effective and have the advantage that you can arrange them on the cake well in advance.

SWEETS AND CANDIES

Novel-shaped sweets can make light work of cake decorating, so keep an eye out for interesting ones that you can use for decorations, particularly for 'seasonal' cakes. Boiled sweets are really effective when melted, cooled and broken-up, as seen in the Jagged Jewel Cake (see page 104).

PAINTED DECORATIONS

If you like painting and have a steady hand, you'll find painting decorations on the cake with food colouring and a fine artist's paintbrush really rewarding. If there's time, let the icing set first so that it won't dent if you rest your hand on it for support.

Something for everyone

Football boots

serves 14
decoration time 30 minutes

2 x 20 cm (8 inch) bought or homemade
   Swiss Rolls (see page 12)

2 tablespoons smooth apricot jam

icing sugar, for dusting

500 g (1 lb) black ready-to-roll icing

125 g (4 oz) grey ready-to-roll icing

125 g (4 oz) white ready-to-roll icing

3 flat liquorice bootlaces

large tissue-lined shoe box

about 10 foil-wrapped chocolate footballs

tip

If you prefer, alter the colours and design
of the boots to personalize the cake. With
minor alterations they'd also make good
rugby boots.

1 Use a small, sharp knife to round off 2 ends of each of the Swiss rolls to make the heels. Out of the top of each cake scoop an oval, about 10 x 5 cm (4 x 2 inches) and 2 cm (¾ inch) deep in the centre. Make a sloping cut from the front of the scooped-out area down to the front end of each cake. Round off all the edges. Brush the jam over the cakes.

2 Dust your work surface with icing sugar and roll out half the black icing to a rectangle, 30 x 20 cm (12 x 8 inches). Lay the icing over one cake, pressing it down into the cavity. Ease the icing to fit around the sides and tuck the ends under the boot. Dust the palms of your hands with icing sugar and smooth the icing. Cover the other cake with the remaining black icing in the same way.

3 Roll out half the grey icing into 2 ovals, each 11 x 6 cm (4½ x 2½ inches), and press them into the cavities in the tops of the boots. Halve the reserved grey icing and shape 2 'boot tongues', each about 12 cm (5 inches) long and 6 cm (2½ inches) across the top. Use a dampened paintbrush to secure them in position. (If the ends of the flaps flop into the cavity, prop them up with some crumpled kitchen paper until the icing has hardened.)

4 Roll out the white icing and cut it into long strips about 2 cm (¾ inch) wide. Arrange them on the boots, rounding off the corners at the front and tucking the ends around the back.

5 Cut the liquorice into 14 pieces, each about 4 cm (1¾ inches) long, and use them for the laces, making holes in the white icing so that you can easily press in the ends. Use longer lengths of liquorice for the trailing ends.

6 Line a shoe box with tissue paper and arrange the boots in the box. Scatter the foil-wrapped footballs around the cakes.

Golfer's bag

serves 16
decoration time 30 minutes plus drying

1 Roll 5 balls, each 25 g (1 oz), of white icing and gently indent each with the end of a paintbrush to make golf balls. Shape the heads of 5 clubs, each 40 g (1½ oz), in white icing, adding markings with a knife. Dampen the tips of the dowelling rods and press them into the ends. Shape several small tees in red icing. Leave them with the clubs and golf balls on a sheet of baking parchment to dry overnight.

2 Dust your work surface with icing sugar and roll out the green icing. Use it to cover the cake board, trimming off the excess.

3 Cut the cakes in half horizontally and sandwich them together into a stack with the buttercream. Put the stacked cakes on the board and spread the jam over the top and sides.

4 Reserve 100 g (3½ oz) of the brown icing. Roll out a further 100 g (3½ oz) of the brown icing to a circle, 15 cm (6 inches) across, and lay it over the top cake. Roll out the remainder and cut out a rectangle, 50 x 16 cm (20 x 6½ inches). Dampen the short edges and wrap it around the cake so that the top edge is about 2 cm (¾ inch) higher than the cakes. Smooth the join together.

5 Roll out the reserved brown icing and cut out a rectangle, 12 x 10 cm (5 x 4 inches). Dampen the edges and secure it to the bag for a pocket. Cut out a strip, 15 x 2 cm (6 x ¾ inch), and secure the ends to the bag for a handle.

6 Use the writing icing to pipe stitches over the bag. Arrange the golf balls and tees beside it.

7 Paint the clubs and rods with silver food colouring and leave to dry. Press them gently into the top of the cake and paint the backs. Secure the ribbon around the edge of the board.

375 g (12 oz) white ready-to-roll icing

5 x 15 cm (6 inch) lengths wood or plastic dowelling

15 g (½ oz) red ready-to-roll icing

icing sugar, for dusting

150 g (5 oz) green ready-to-roll icing

23 cm (9 inch) round cake board

2 x 15 cm (6 inch) round bought or homemade Madeira Cakes (see page 11)

single quantity Buttercream (see page 16)

3 tablespoons smooth apricot jam

1 kg (2 lb) brown ready-to-roll icing

1 tube black writing icing

silver food colouring

red ribbon for edge of cake board

tip
Wood or plastic dowelling rods are available from cake decorating shops and from DIY stores. If you buy long sticks, cut them to size before using.

The one that got away

serves 8
decoration time 30 minutes

18 cm (7 inch) square bought or homemade
   Madeira Cake (see page 11)

wooden board, at least 45 x 15 cm
   (18 x 6 inches)

3 tablespoons smooth apricot jam

icing sugar, for dusting

500 g (1 lb) pale blue ready-to-roll icing

100 g (3½ oz) white ready-to-roll icing

15 g (½ oz) black ready-to-roll icing

pink food colouring or powder

black food colouring

silver food colouring powder

tip

Silver food colouring powder is perfect for
adding a pearly finish to the icing. Use a
dry brush or the sheen will be patchy.

1 Shape the fish by cutting the cake in half vertically and placing
the pieces end to end on the work surface. Use a small, sharp
knife to cut a fish body shape out of the cake. Ignore the mouth,
fins and tail, which will be added later. Remember that the head
end of the fish is much larger than the tail end. Transfer the fish
shape to the board and spread the jam over the surface.

2 Dust your work surface with icing sugar and roll out the blue
icing to an oval, 35 x 15 cm (14 x 6 inches). Lift it over the fish.
Smooth the icing around the sides of the cake and trim off the
excess around the base.

3 Use the white icing to shape the tail, fins and mouth, adding
tail and fin markings with the tip of a knife. Shape a small,
round eye in white and black icing.

4 Thin a little pink food colouring with water or mix a little pink
powder with water and use it to paint a thick band of colour
down the centre of the fish and inside the mouth. Use the black
food colouring and a fine paintbrush to paint the mouth and fins
and a design on the back. Use a dry paintbrush to brush a little
silver powder down the centre of the fish and over the mouth.

First prize

serves 24
decoration time about 1 hour

23 cm (9 inch) square bought or homemade
   Madeira Cake (see page 11)

6 tablespoons smooth strawberry or
   raspberry jam

single quantity Buttercream (see page 16)

45 x 30 cm (18 x 12 inch) rectangular cake
   board or tray

1.25 kg (2½ lb) white ready-to-roll icing

icing sugar, for dusting

50 g (2 oz) brown ready-to-roll icing

200 g (7 oz) grey ready-to-roll icing

black food colouring

gold food colouring

1 metre (39 inches) red ribbon, about 3 cm
   (1¼ inches) wide

red rosette

red ribbon for edges of cake board

tips

Cut the cake into perfectly even thicknesses
to make a good base for the icing.
   Serve at a celebration for any sporting
triumph – tennis, swimming, golf or horse-
riding – and use the appropriate team
colours. Paint names or a message on
the stand.

1 Slice any dome off the top of the cake. Using a ruler as a guide, cut the cake vertically in half. Cut each half into 3 equal vertical slices and lay the slices together on their sides to make one large rectangle. Cut horizontally through the whole rectangle. Use the buttercream and half the jam to sandwich the cakes together, re-assembling them in the rectangle on the board. Spread the remaining jam over the top and sides of the cake.

2 Reserve 200 g (7 oz) of the white icing. Dust your work surface with icing sugar and roll out the remainder of the white icing to a rectangle that will cover the cake. Lift it over the cake, easing it down the sides and trimming off the excess around the base.

3 Make the trophy by rolling out the brown icing to a rectangle, 7.5 x 5 cm (3 x 2 inches), and place it on the top of the cake for the trophy stand, using a dampened paintbrush to secure it in position. Cut out a square of greaseproof paper, 10 x 10 cm (4 x 4 inches), and round off 2 corners to make the shape of a goblet. Roll out a small piece of grey icing and cut out a trophy base, about 5 cm (2 inches) deep and with curved sides. Secure it to the stand. Using the greaseproof paper shape as a template, cut out the goblet shape and secure in position. Roll out the remaining grey icing under the palms of your hands into thin ropes and bend them into handles and trimmings for the trophy base.

4 Lightly knead dots of black food colouring into the reserved white icing to make a marbled effect. Use this to cover the edges of the cake board, trimming off the excess around the edges.

5 Use the gold food colouring to add highlights to the trophy and stand. Secure the ribbon around the sides of the cake and position the rosette beside one of the handles. Secure more ribbon around the edges of the cake board.

Green fingers

serves 20
decoration time 30 minutes plus drying

1 Make the trowel by rolling the purple icing into a thick sausage. Flatten the ends and use the back of a small knife to indent markings at each end. Press 2 cocktail sticks, slightly apart, into one end. Flatten the grey icing into a scoop shape with one straight edge. Press the cocktail sticks into the straight edge and rest the trowel over a foil-covered rolling pin to harden for about 24 hours.

2 Cut the cake in half horizontally and sandwich it with all but 1 tablespoon of the buttercream and half the jam. Place it on the board. Use a dessertspoon to scoop out a little of the centre of the cake and pack it into the pot. Spread it with the reserved buttercream and sprinkle with a little of the grated chocolate. Scoop out a little more of the cake to make a wider cavity. Spread the remaining jam over the top and sides of the cake.

3 Dust your work surface with icing sugar and roll out the green icing to a circle, 35 cm (14 inches) across. Lay it over the cake, easing it into the cavity and around the sides and letting the excess icing rest on the board.

4 Press the bay and a few lavender sprigs into the cake in the pot. Arrange more sprigs around the sides of the cake, securing them in the icing on the board.

5 Scatter a pile of grated chocolate over the top of the cake and in piles around the sides. Position the pot and trowel on top of the cake.

50 g (2 oz) purple ready-to-roll icing

2 cocktail sticks

50 g (2 oz) grey ready-to-roll icing

23 cm (9 inch) round bought or homemade Madeira Cake (see page 11)

single quantity Buttercream (see page 16)

6 tablespoons smooth raspberry or strawberry jam

30–35 cm (12–14 inch) round wooden board

small terracotta pot, about 6 cm (2½ inches) in diameter

100 g (3½ oz) plain chocolate, finely grated

icing sugar, for dusting

1 kg (2 lb) green ready-to-roll icing

icing sugar, for dusting

1 small sprig of bay leaves

plenty of small sprigs of lavender leaves and flowers

tip

Herbs and herb flowers make pretty decorations and won't wilt as quickly as other fresh flowers, so if you use them you can assemble the cake a day in advance. Alternatively, use other small flowers, such as rose buds, primroses or geraniums, and position them at the last minute.

Graduation cake

serves 20
preparation and cooking time about 1½ hours
decoration time 1 hour

6-egg quantity Madeira Cake mixture
(see page 11)

single quantity Buttercream (see page 16)

3 tablespoons smooth apricot jam

250 g (8 oz) ivory-coloured ready-to-roll
icing

icing sugar, for dusting

1 kg (2 lb) purple ready-to-roll icing

30 x 25 cm (12 x 10 inch) wooden board

75 g (3 oz) chocolate brown ready-to-roll
icing

50 g (2 oz) yellow ready-to-roll icing

1 tube yellow writing icing

gold food colouring

tips

Purple icing can be made by kneading
Grape Violet food colouring into white
ready-to-roll icing or by kneading together
red and blue ready-to-roll icings until you
get the right colour.

You can add a name or message to the
plaque on the spine of the book.

1 Turn the cake mixture into a greased and lined cake tin,
23 cm (9 inches) square. Bake in a preheated oven, 160°C
(325°F), Gas Mark 3, for 1–1¼ hours until just firm and a skewer
inserted into the centre comes out clean. Leave to cool. Slice any
dome off the top of the cake. Cut a slice, 5 cm (2 inches) wide, off
one side and position it at one end of the larger piece. Trim off the
excess to make a rectangle. Cut the cake in half horizontally and
sandwich it with the buttercream, securing the smaller piece of
cake to the larger one with more buttercream.

2 Use a sharp knife to round off the corners of one long side.
Cut curves into the other long side and the ends to make a
book shape. Spread the 3 curved sides with a little apricot jam.
Reserve a little of the ivory-coloured icing. Roll out the remainder
to a long strip, the depth of the cake and the length of the 3 sides.
Press it into position and score it with a knife.

3 Roll out a scant half of the purple icing to a rectangle about
1 cm (½ inch) longer and 1 cm (½ inch) wider than the cake.
Place it on the board and position the cake on top so that the ivory-
coloured icing sits about 5 mm (¼ inch) away from the edges of the
purple icing. Roll out the remaining purple icing to the same length
but add an extra 5 cm (2 inches) to the width to cover the 'spine' of
the book. Position it on the cake, tucking the ends under the spine.

4 Use the reserved ivory-coloured icing to make the owl's head
and body and secure to the cake with a dampened paintbrush.
Use the yellow icing for eyes and claws and the brown icing for
wings, the top of the head, the beak and centres of the eyes.
Position 2 more rectangles of brown icing on the spine. Pipe yellow
icing around the edges and spine of the book and around the owl's
wings. Dab spots of gold paint on the owl's breast.

Bon voyage

serves 20
decoration time 30 minutes

1 Slice any dome off the top of the cake. Cut a slice 8 cm (3¼ inches) wide off the cake and then cut off (and discard) one-third of the slice to leave 2 rectangular pieces. Halve each horizontally and sandwich with buttercream. Place the larger cake on the tray or board and brush both cakes with apricot jam.

2 Dust your work surface with icing sugar and roll out two-thirds of the red icing to a rectangle, 10 cm (4 inches) longer and wider than the large cake. Lay the icing over the cake, smoothing the icing down the sides and trimming off the excess around the base. Cover the small cake with the remaining red icing and place it on the large cake.

3 Roll out a thin strip of white icing and trim it to a strip 1 cm (½ inch) wide and long enough to go around the small cake. Lightly dampen the back of the strip and secure it in position. Use a larger strip to wrap around the large cake. Run the tip of a knife along each strip to make an indentation. Cut out small rectangles of icing and position 2 rectangles on the small case at either side of the strip and 2 on the large case. Add smaller rectangles of icing for the clasps.

4 Roll 2 pieces of icing, each 40 g (1½ oz), into sausage shapes and bend the ends over to shape handles. Secure them in position. Paint the clasps with silver food colouring.

23 cm (9 inch) square bought or homemade Madeira Cake (see page 11)

single quantity Buttercream (see page 16)

large metal tray or 28 cm (11 inch) square cake board

3 tablespoons smooth apricot jam

icing sugar, for dusting

1 kg (2 lb) deep red ready-to-roll icing

200 g (7 oz) white ready-to-roll icing

silver food colouring

tips

If you're throwing a large party for someone about to set off on their travels, you could use a rich fruit cake instead of a Madeira cake. If you do, cover it with almond paste before icing.

As a finishing touch, write the recipient's name and destination on a luggage label and attach it to one of the handles.

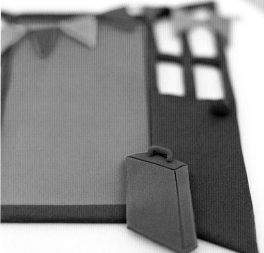

Welcome home

serves 40
decoration time 1 hour

25 cm (10 inch) round Rich Fruit Cake,
   covered with almond paste (see pages
   14 and 23 for recipe and technique)

30 cm (12 inch) round cake board

icing sugar, for dusting

1 kg (2 lb) white ready-to-roll icing

75 g (3 oz) each of orange, chocolate
   brown, green, red and blue ready-to-roll
   icing

1 tube red writing icing

red ribbon for edge of cake board

tips

Use the writing icing tube to write a
message – the recipient's name or
'Welcome', for example – on the bunting
on top of the cake.

   If you're not used to writing with icing,
practise on a sheet of greaseproof paper.

1 Place the cake on the board. Dust your work surface with icing
   sugar and roll out the white icing to a circle, 38 cm (15 inches)
across. Lay it over the cake, smoothing the icing around the sides
and trimming off the excess around the base.

2 Roll out a little of the orange icing and trim to a rectangle,
   12 x 7 cm (5 x 2¾ inches). Dampen the underside lightly with
water and place it on top of the cake. Roll out the brown icing and
cut out 2 strips, 5 mm (¼ inch) wide and each the width of the
orange rectangle. Position one strip at each end of the orange
icing. Cut out 2 more rectangles, 17 x 3 cm (6½ x 1¼ inches), from
the brown icing. Lay them against the long sides of the orange icing
and trim off the ends at angles to represent open doors. Cut out
windows in the top half of the doors if liked and add 2 door knobs.

3 Pipe scallops of red writing icing around the sides of the cake
   and at the top of the doors. Thinly roll out a little orange,
green, red and blue icing and cut them into strips 2 cm (¾ inch)
wide. From each strip cut out triangles for bunting. Dampen the
pieces with water and secure them to the cake. Use red icing to
cover the edges of the cake board.

4 Shape a small case in blue icing and place it on top of the cake
   next to the open doors. Write a message on the bunting if liked
and secure the red ribbon around the edge of the board.

Chocobloc

serves 8–10
decoration time 30 minutes

15 cm (6 inch) square bought or homemade
Rich Chocolate Cake (see page 13)

single quantity Dark Chocolate Ganache
(see page 18)

35 x 28 cm (14 x 11 inches) rectangular
marble slab or cake board

plenty of gold foil (e.g., chocolate bar
wrappings)

icing sugar, for dusting

250 g (8 oz) purple ready-to-roll icing

tip

Cover the parts of the cake that won't be
hidden under icing or foil with the ganache
first, before it starts to thicken. Slide a piece
of greaseproof paper under the wire rack to
catch the ganache that falls through – you
can scrape it up and spread it over areas of
the cake that won't be visible.

1 Slice any dome off the top of the cake. Cut a slice 8 cm
(3¼ inches) wide off the cake and then cut off (and discard)
one-third of the slice to leave 2 rectangular pieces. Halve each
horizontally and sandwich with buttercream. Place the larger cake
on the tray or board and brush both cakes with apricot jam.

2 While the ganache is still fairly runny, spoon a little over the
cake pieces, spreading it down the sides so they are completely
covered. Leave for about 10 minutes to firm up a little, then cover
with the remaining ganache.

3 Transfer the chocolate bar to the marble or board and cut-off
a few pieces.

4 Wrap one end of the chocolate cake in a strip of the gold foil.
Dust your work surface with icing sugar and roll out the purple
icing to a rectangle, 22 x 14 cm (8¾ x 5½ inches). Lay it over the
cake so that one edge rests over the foil strip. Tear more foil into
jagged pieces and tuck under the other end of the icing.

5 Shape the icing trimmings and a little more gold foil into 'torn'
wrappings and scatter them around the cake.

Chocolate truffle cake

serves 18
decoration time 30 minutes

20 cm (8 inch) round bought or homemade
   Rich Chocolate Cake (see page 13)

25–28 cm (10–11 inch) round plate

3 x 120 g (4½ oz) packs chocolate sticks

single quantity Dark Chocolate Ganache or
   double quantity Chocolate Fudge Icing
   (see page 18 or 19)

300 g (10 oz) bought or homemade
   chocolate truffles (see tip)

50 g (2 oz) pink crystallized roses

1.5 metres (5 feet) pink ribbon, 4–5 cm
   (1½–2 inches) wide

1 Trim the chocolate sticks so that they are 1 cm (½ inch) longer than the depth of the cake. Place the cake on the plate and use a palette knife to spread the ganache or fudge icing over the top and sides.

2 While the icing is still soft, secure the chocolate sticks, spacing them fractionally apart, around the sides of the cake.

3 Arrange the truffles over the top of the cake and scatter over the roses. Tie the ribbon around the cake, finishing with a bow.

tip

If you prefer to make your own chocolate truffles, heat 125 ml (4 fl oz) double cream in a small pan until it bubbles around the edges. Remove it from the heat and stir in 250 g (8 oz) chopped plain chocolate. Leave until the chocolate has melted, then turn the mixture into a bowl and flavour it with 2 tablespoons orange or coffee liqueur, brandy or rum. Chill until firm enough to roll into small balls and dust with cocoa powder.

Feathered hat

serves 12
decoration time 30 minutes

2 x 15 cm (6 inch) round bought or
    homemade Madeira Cakes (see page 11)

single quantity Buttercream (see page 16)

6 tablespoons smooth raspberry or
    strawberry jam

28 cm (11 inch) round cake board

icing sugar, for dusting

1 kg (2 lb) ivory-coloured ready-to-roll icing

50 cm (20 inches) bottle green wired
    ribbon, about 7.5 cm (3 inches) wide

spray of dark green feathers

large ivory-coloured silk flower

ivory-coloured ribbon for edge of cake board

tip

This makes a great birthday cake for a
friend who's crazy about hats. Use any
colour theme you prefer for the icing and
decorations, which can be as traditional
or as flamboyant as you like.

1 Cut a slice off the top of each cake so they are about 5 cm
(2 inches) deep. Cut each cake in half horizontally and sandwich
the 4 layers together with half the buttercream and all the jam.
Place the cake towards one side of the cake board and spread the
remaining buttercream over the top and sides.

2 Dust your work surface with icing sugar and roll out 750 g
(1½ lb) of the ivory-coloured icing to a circle, 28 cm (11 inches)
across. Lift it over the cake and smooth the icing down the sides,
trimming off any excess around the base.

3 Dampen the board with a little water. Combine the trimmings
with the remaining icing and use it to cover the cake board.
The easiest way to do this is to roll out the icing into a thick, curved
crescent shape, roughly the same size as the exposed board area.
Trim the inner curve of the crescent and lift the icing around the
cake, smoothing it out to fit the board and trimming off the excess
around the edges.

4 Make a loop in the centre of the green ribbon and tuck it to one
side of the cake, bending the wired ends of the ribbon up over
the cake. Secure it to the iced board with a little clear tape. Position
the feathers and silk flower against the side of the cake, pressing
them gently into the icing. Secure the ivory-coloured ribbon around
the edge of the cake board.

Vase of flowers

serves 12
preparation and cooking time about 1 hour
decoration time 20 minutes

1 Turn the cake mixture into a greased and lined cake tin, 20 cm (8 inches) square, and level the surface. Bake in a preheated oven, 160°C (325°F), Gas Mark 3, for about 45 minutes or until just firm and a skewer, inserted in the centre comes out clean. Leave to cool.

2 Slice the domed surface off the top of the cake and cut it into 4 equal pieces. Use half the buttercream to stack the cakes together. Transfer the cakes to the plate and spread the remaining buttercream over the top and sides with a palette knife.

3 Dust your work surface with icing sugar and roll out the red icing. Cut out 4 rectangles, each 1 cm (½ inch) longer than the depth of the cake and 11 cm (4½ inches) wide. Position a rectangle against each side of the cake, dampening the edges with a paintbrush so they stick together.

4 Cut the rose stems to 5 cm (2 inches) long and wrap the ends in clingfilm or foil. Press them into the top of the cake. Leave the icing to harden for a couple of hours or overnight, then wrap the raffia loosely around the sides of the cake.

4-egg quantity Madeira Cake mixture (see page 11)

double quantity Buttercream (see page 16)

square plate

icing sugar, for dusting

750 g (1½ lb) deep red ready-to-roll icing

small bunch dried roses

plenty of raffia

tip

Serving a tall cake like this can be awkward. It will be easier if you remove the raffia and flowers and then split the cake in half horizontally to make two regular-shaped cakes, which you can then serve cut into squares.

New parents

serves 24
decoration time 1 hour

15 cm (6 inch) and 20 cm (8 inch) round
   bought or homemade Madeira Cakes
   (see page 11)

double quantity Buttercream (see page 16)

8 tablespoons lemon or orange curd

25–28 cm (10–11 inch) round or square plate

icing sugar, for dusting

1.3 kg (2¾ lb) pale pink or blue ready-to-roll
   icing

25 g (1 oz) flesh-coloured ready-to-roll icing

50 g (2 oz) deep pink or blue ready-to-roll
   icing

blue food colouring

50 g (2 oz) white ready-to-roll icing

50 g (2 oz) yellow ready-to-roll icing

small plastic cake decorations (e.g., nappy
   pins, rattles)

50 g (2 oz) pink and yellow dolly-mixture
   candies

tip

This makes a fabulous gift for new parents,
who can indulge in it themselves or serve it
to the stream of visitors who'll come to
admire their baby. It would also make a
good christening cake if you're looking for
something a bit different.

1 Cut each cake in half horizontally and sandwich them together
with half the buttercream and the lemon or orange curd. Spread
the remaining buttercream over the top and sides of the cakes.
Place the larger cake on the plate.

2 Dust your work surface with icing sugar and roll out two-thirds
of the pink or blue icing to a circle, 33 cm (13 inches) across,
and cover the larger cake, smoothing the icing down the sides and
trimming off the excess around the base. Roll out the remaining
icing to a circle, 28 cm (11 inches) across, and cover the smaller
cake. Position the smaller cake on the centre of the larger one.

3 Roll a small ball of flesh-coloured icing for baby's head,
adding a small button nose. Shape hands and feet with more
flesh-coloured icing. Roll the deep pink or blue icing into an oval
and flatten it slightly with the palm of your hand. Make 2 cuts for
the arms and one for the legs (see the illustration). Smooth out the
edges and cut off the tips. Make button markings with the tip of
a paintbrush. Secure to the top of the cake with a dampened
paintbrush, bending the shape into a sitting-up position. Secure the
head, hands and feet and add features with the blue colouring and
a fine paintbrush.

4 Shape feeding bottles from the remaining icing and secure
them around the cake with the plastic cake decorations.
Scatter plenty of small candies around the tiers.

Animal ark

serves 28
decoration time about 1½ hours

3 x 340 g (12 oz) packs of fun-size flaked chocolate bars

12 cm (5 inch) and 18 cm (7 inch) square bought or homemade Rich Chocolate Cakes (see page 13)

triple quantity Chocolate Buttercream (see page 16)

25 cm (10 inch) square plate

icing sugar, for dusting

200 g (7 oz) pink ready-to-roll icing

200 g (7 oz) chocolate brown ready-to-roll icing

200 g (7 oz) light brown ready-to-roll icing

200 g (7 oz) yellow ready-to-roll icing

black food colouring

tips

Rich and chocolatey, this cake would make a great 'alternative' christening cake and would be especially appealing to younger guests.

The animals are a bit fiddly, but you can make them several weeks in advance and store them in an airtight container, so that you can complete the cake a couple of days in advance.

1 Trim the flaked chocolate bars to 1 cm (½ inch) longer than the cakes. Cut each cake into 3 layers and sandwich with buttercream. Place the larger cake on the plate and spread with more buttercream. Position the smaller cake on top and spread with the remaining buttercream.

2 Use a fine-bladed knife and carefully cut each chocolate bar in half. Position them around the sides of the cakes.

3 To make each elephant roll a small ball of pink icing into an oval. Press it into the buttercream. Take a larger ball of icing and mould a flattened pear shape, gradually elongating the thin end into a trunk. Cut off the tip of the trunk and impress lines along it with a knife. Prop the icing against the pink base, securing with a dampened paintbrush. Shape and secure large floppy ears.

4 To make each monkey roll a small ball of chocolate brown icing for the head and press it into the buttercream. Shape large round ears and secure them to the sides of the head. Secure a flattened ball of light brown icing for the snout.

5 To make each lion roll a small ball of yellow icing into an oval and press it into the buttercream. Flatten a piece of brown icing for the mane and indent it around the edges with your fingertips. Roll another ball of icing and flatten it against the mane. Position it on the yellow base. Add ears and a thin rope of icing for the tail.

6 To make each bear roll a small ball of light brown icing into an oval and press it into the buttercream. Roll a larger ball of icing and position it for the head, adding 2 small, round ears. Secure a flattened ball of icing for the snout. Use the icing trimmings to add paws, and a fine paintbrush and black food colouring to add features to the animals' faces.

Man's best friend

serves 24
decoration time about 1 hour

1 Halve the cake horizontally and sandwich the pieces together with one-third of the chocolate fudge icing. Put it on the plate and use a palette knife to swirl the remainder of the fudge icing over the top and sides of the cake.

2 To shape the dog, roll a 200 g (7 oz) ball of brown icing for the body and flatten it slightly. Place it on the centre of the cake. Roll a 175g (6oz) ball of icing for the head. Pinch one side to a point to make a snout. Rest the head, tilting it slightly to one side, at one end of the 'body'. From the remaining icing shape small paws, droopy ears and a curved tail. Position the paws and ears and reserve the tail.

3 Dust your work surface with icing sugar and thinly roll out the blue icing. Cut out a 20 cm (8 inch) square. Drape the icing over the cake, fitting it first around the dog's head and draping it across the cake in loose folds. Position the tail.

4 Use a fine paintbrush and the blue or black food colouring to paint closed eyes, a snout and a mouth on the dog's face.

25 cm (10 inch) round bought or homemade Madeira Cake or Rich Chocolate Cake (see pages 11 or 13)

triple quantity Chocolate Fudge Icing (see page 19)

30 cm (12 inch) round plate

425 g (14 oz) light brown ready-to-roll icing

icing sugar, for dusting

200 g (7 oz) blue ready-to-roll icing

dark blue or black food colouring

tip

It's not only children who like animal cakes – there are plenty of adults who would find this cake appealing. The dog can easily be 'personalized' to resemble the recipient's own dog by changing the colour of the icing and by painting on spots or patches as appropriate.

First night

serves 24
decoration time 1 hour plus drying

icing sugar, for dusting

1.25 kg (2½ lb) white ready-to-roll icing

25 cm (10 inch) round bought or
   homemade Madeira Cake (see page 11)

single quantity Buttercream (see page 16)

6 tablespoons raspberry or strawberry jam

30–35 cm (12–14 inch) round plate,
   preferably gold or red

50 cm (19½ inches) fine red cord

50 cm (19½ inches) fine gold cord

425 g (14 oz) red ready-to-roll icing

50 g (2 oz) purple ready-to-roll icing

gold food colouring

tip

This is a brilliant cake for budding actors.
The masks are far easier to make than
they look and can be made well in advance
so they have plenty of time to harden.
Make a spare one of each – just in case
of breakages.

1 Wrap a piece of baking parchment around a tall tumbler and prop it up at either side with a little icing. To make the mask templates cut out 2 rectangles, each 10 x 7.5 cm (4 x 3 inches), from greaseproof paper and fold them in half lengthways. Round off the lower half of the masks from halfway along the sides to the point of the folded edge. Gently curve the top edge of the masks from the folded point to the sides. Cut out eyes. Cut a smiling mouth on one mask a sad one on the other.

2 Dust your work surface with icing sugar and roll out 100 g (3½ oz) of the white icing. Lay the templates over the icing and cut out the mask shapes. Carefully transfer them to the tumbler so they set in a curved shape. Leave them for 24 hours.

3 Cut the cake in half horizontally and sandwich it with half the buttercream and all the jam. Place it on the plate and spread the top and sides with the remaining buttercream.

4 Roll out the remaining white icing to a circle, 35 cm (14 inches) across, and cover the cake, smoothing the icing around the sides and trimming off the excess around the base.

5 Halve the red icing and thinly roll one half to a rectangle, about 28 x 12 cm (11 x 5 inches). Drape the icing over one side of the cake, pinching it together slightly in the centre to resemble curtains. Use a dampened paintbrush to secure the red icing to the white so it doesn't slip around. Secure two lengths of cord around the icing then make the other curtain in the same way. Cut out thin strips of purple icing, about 5 mm (¼ inch) wide, and secure them around the edges of the curtains.

6 Carefully peel the paper away from the masks and paint them gold. Position them, slightly overlapping, on top of the cake.

Hearts and flowers

A glittery engagement

serves 20
decoration time 30 minutes

1 Cut the larger cake in half horizontally and sandwich it with the jam and a little of the buttercream. Put the cake on the plate and spread the top and sides with half the remaining buttercream, spreading it in an even layer with a palette knife.

2 Cut the smaller cake in half horizontally and put one half on the large cake. Spread with more buttercream. Using a small cup or glass as a guide, cut out a circle, 7.5 cm (3 inches) across, from the other piece of cake. Put it on top of the cake and spread it with the remaining buttercream.

3 Gently press the ring on to the top of the cake. Use the remaining jewellery to decorate the sides of the cake (see tip).

15 cm (6 inch) and 18 cm (7 inch) round
bought or homemade Madeira Cakes
(see page 11)

4 tablespoons raspberry or strawberry jam

quadruple quantity Buttercream
(see page 16)

23 cm (9 inch) round plate

selection of 'fake' diamanté jewellery
including a large ring (see tip)

tip

This cake is a wonderful idea for a small engagement celebration. A browse around inexpensive jewellery shops should unearth an inspiring range of diamanté-type decorations, the sparklier the better!

The way you drape them around the cake will depend on their length and style: long necklaces can be put around the bottom of the cake or arranged in a series of scallops around the tiers, and bracelets and earrings can be arranged as individual decorations. Just remember to remove all the jewellery before serving and to wash it thoroughly both before and after use.

Winter wedding cake

serves 50–55
decoration time 1 hour plus drying

15 cm (6 inch) and 25 cm (10 inch) round bought or homemade Rich Fruit Cakes, covered with almond paste (see pages 14 and 23 for recipe and technique)

35–40 cm (14–16 inch) round glass platter or cake stand

double quantity Royal Icing (see page 19)

1 egg white, lightly beaten

12 rosemary sprigs, about 6 cm (2½ inches) long

8 bay leaf sprigs

caster and icing sugar, for dusting

8 small fir cones

100 g (3½ oz) sugar cubes

6 tea lights

1 Put the larger cake on the platter and spread two-thirds of the royal icing over it, swirling it in an even layer with a palette knife. Place the smaller cake on top and cover it with the remaining icing.

2 To frost the herb sprigs, put the lightly beaten egg white in a bowl. Use your fingers to coat a rosemary sprig with egg white so that it's evenly moistened but not dripping. Dip the sprig into caster sugar and transfer it to a tray covered with baking parchment. Leave it to dry for at least 1 hour. Coat the remaining rosemary and the bay leaf sprigs in the same way.

3 Using a tea strainer, generously dust the fir cones with icing sugar. Put the sugar cubes into a plastic bag and tap them gently with a rolling pin until they are broken into smaller pieces.

4 Dust the platter with icing sugar. Position 2 tea lights on the top tier and 4 on the lower tier. Arrange the herbs and fir cones around the tea lights and scatter the pieces of sugar to fill the gaps between the decorations and around the lower tier. Cover loosely and store in a cool place for up to 1 week.

tip

This cake will make a great centrepiece for your Christmas table or for a winter wedding anniversary or birthday party. Don't forget to light the tea lights for a truly stunning effect!

White chocolate wedding cake

serves 30–35
decoration time 1½ hours

400 g (13 oz) white chocolate

25 g (1 oz) unsalted butter

15 cm (6 inch) and 25 cm (10 inch) round bought or homemade Rich Chocolate Cakes (see page 13)

30–35 cm (12–14 inch) round glass or frosted glass platter

triple quantity White Chocolate Ganache (see page 18)

12–14 white freesias

8–10 white or coral pink ranunculus

6–8 white or cream lisianthus

tip

Chocolate curls – caraque – are stunning cake decorations and are easy to make once you've got the hang of the technique.

The curls can be made a couple of weeks in advance and kept in a cool place or in the refrigerator.

The day before the wedding, complete the cake up to the end of step 4, leaving only the flowers to arrange on the day.

1 Break the white chocolate into pieces and put them in a bowl with the butter. Place the bowl over a saucepan of gently simmering water and leave it until the chocolate has melted. Gently stir the chocolate to incorporate the butter. Tip the mixture on to a piece of marble or glass or a thoroughly clean plastic chopping board and spread it to a thin, even layer. Leave in a cool place or in the refrigerator until set.

2 When the chocolate is just set, draw a fine-bladed knife across it at an angle of 45 degrees to pare off long chocolate curls. If the chocolate breaks off in brittle shavings it's too cold, so leave it at room temperature for a few minutes and try again. If the chocolate is sticky and clings to the knife put it in the refrigerator for about 10 minutes and then try again.

3 Put the larger cake on the platter and spread two-thirds of the ganache over it. While the ganache is still soft press the chocolate curls vertically into it. You needn't be too precise or careful about doing this – the more casually it's done, the better the finished result.

4 Position the small cake and cover it with the remaining ganache. Press more chocolate curls around the sides. Keep the cake in a cool place or in the refrigerator until ready to serve.

5 Cut the stems of all the flowers short and use them to decorate the tops of the cakes.

Chocolate wedding cake

serves 34
decoration time 1½ hours

1 Cut both cakes in half horizontally and sandwich them together with half the chocolate fudge icing. Put the smaller cake on the 20 cm (8 inch) board and the larger cake on the 30 cm (12 inch) board. Spread the top and sides of the cakes with the remaining icing.

2 Dust your work surface with icing sugar and roll out 1 kg (2 lb) of the icing to a circle, 35 cm (14 inches) across. Lift the icing over the larger cake. Smooth the icing down the sides and trim off the excess around the base. Reserve the trimmings.

3 Roll out a further 750 g (1½ lb) of the icing and use it to cover the smaller cake. Knead the trimmings and remaining icing together. Secure the 2 largest cake boards together with clear tape, then secure the large cake, on its board, on top.

4 Cover all the top edges of the cake boards with the remaining icing, starting with the smallest and working down to the largest board. Rest the smaller cake on top of the larger one. Wrap the coffee-coloured ribbon around the cakes. Secure the ivory-coloured ribbon around all the boards.

5 Pile the chocolates on top of the smaller cake and around the edge of the larger one. Scatter the coffee beans on top.

15 cm (6 inch) round and 25 cm (10 inch) round bought or homemade Rich Chocolate Cakes (see page 13)

triple quantity Chocolate Fudge Icing (see page 19)

20 cm (8 inch), 30 cm (12 inch), 33 cm (13 inch) and 35 cm (14 inch) round cake boards

icing sugar, for dusting

2 kg (4 lb) chocolate brown ready-to-roll icing

1.5 metres (5 feet) coffee-coloured ribbon, 4 cm (1½ inches) wide

4 metres (13 feet) white ribbon for edges of cake boards

500 g (1 lb) box of chocolates

100 g (3½ oz) mixed chocolate coffee beans

tip

If you're transporting this cake to a special event keep the tiers separate until you get there and assemble the cake in its final position, scattering with the chocolates and coffee beans at the last minute.

Ribbony chocolate wedding cake

serves 50
decoration time 1 hour plus standing

15 cm (6 inch), 20 cm (8 inch) and 25 cm
(10 inch) round bought or homemade
Rich Chocolate Cakes (see page 13)

triple quantity Dark Chocolate Ganache
(see page 18)

30 cm (12 inch) round cake stand or
glass platter

3 metres (10 feet) wired red ribbon, about
4 cm (1½ inches) wide

3 metres (10 feet) wired lilac or cream
ribbon, about 2.5 cm (1 inch) wide

about 20 small, dried, red, pale green, lilac
or cream-coloured flowers

tips

Before covering the cake layers with
ganache, drizzle them with an orange
or coffee liqueur or with brandy. Allow
about 4 tablespoons for the top tier,
100 ml (3½ fl oz) for the middle tier and
150 ml (¼ pint) for the bottom tier.

If you want to make the cake in
advance, assemble it to the end of step 2
and store overnight in a cool place. Add
the flowers and ribbons the following day.

1 Cut each cake in half horizontally. Use about a quarter of the
ganache to sandwich them together.

2 Place the largest cake on the cake stand or platter and cover
it with a scant half of the ganache, swirling it in an even layer
with a palette knife. Rest the medium-sized cake on top and spread
with more ganache. Position the smallest cake and spread with
the remaining ganache. Leave the cake in a cool place for about
1 hour until the chocolate has firmed up slightly.

3 Wrap the red ribbon around your hand and then uncoil it
loosely around the cake, starting at the top and working
around the cake in a spiral to the bottom. Pressing the edge of the
ribbon gently into the chocolate icing on the top tier should be
sufficient to hold it in place. It can then be secured under the edge
of the cake stand at the other end with a small piece of clear tape.
Create the same effect with the narrower ribbon, keeping the coil
loose and informal.

4 Tuck the flowers, in groups of 2–3, among the coils of
ribbon decoration.

hearts and flowers   71

Layered rose wedding cake

serves 75–80
decoration time 1½ hours

1 Place the cakes on the square boards. Dust your work surface with icing sugar and roll out 1 kg (2 lb) of the icing to a 35 cm (14 inch) square. Lift the icing over the largest cake. Smooth it down the sides and trim off the excess around the base.

2 Cover the medium-sized cake with 750g (1½ lb) of the icing and the small cake with the remainder, each time rolling the icing to a square 12 cm (5 inches) larger than the diameter of the cake.

3 Use clear tape to fasten together the 12 cm (5 inch) boards and the 18 cm (7 inch) boards. Secure the ivory-coloured ribbon around the edges of the boards.

4 To assemble the cake, place the 18 cm (7 inch) stacked cake boards on the large cake and position the medium-sized cake on top. Put the 12 cm (5 inch) stacked cake boards on top of this and position the small cake on top.

5 Cut the rose stems down to 2 cm (¾ inch). Tuck all the roses, closely together, around the 2 bottom tiers, fitting them together so they make an attractive decoration without looking too crammed. Arrange the posy of roses on top of the cake.

12 cm (5 inch), 18 cm (7 inch) and 23 cm (9 inch) square bought or homemade Rich Fruit Cakes, covered with almond paste (see pages 14 and 23 for recipe and technique)

15 cm (6 inch), 20 cm (8 inch) and 28 cm (11 inch) square cake boards, plus 3 x 12 cm (5 inch) and 3 x 18 cm (7 inch) round boards for stacking

icing sugar, for dusting

2.25 kg (5 lb) ivory-coloured ready-to-roll icing

3 metres (10 feet) ivory-coloured ribbon for edges of boards

about 30 pale pink or 30 ivory-coloured open roses or a mixture of the 2 colours

small posy of roses for top of cake

tip

This cake can be prepared up to the end of step 3 several weeks in advance, but the assembly of the roses needs to be done on the day. Set the posy in a shallow bowl of water and wrap the ends of the other roses in moistened cotton wool, then in foil so that water does not seep out over the cake.

Sugared almond wedding cake

serves 20
decoration time 30 minutes

18 cm (7 inch) square homemade Rich
    Fruit Cake (see page 14) or 3 bought
    fruit slab cakes

4 tablespoons smooth apricot jam

25 cm (10 inch) square or 30 cm (12 inch)
    round cake platter or cake stand

icing sugar, for dusting

1.5 kg (3 lb) white ready-to-roll icing

18 cm (7 inch) square silver cake board

1 kg (2 lb) white or coloured sugared
    almonds

2 metres (6 feet) wired ribbon, about
    5 cm (2 inches) wide

silver or white wedding confetti

tips

Don't forget to drizzle the cake with a
few tablespoons of brandy or liqueur
before decorating.
    You may want to cover the cake with
1 kg (2 lb) almond paste (see page 23)
before covering with icing.

1 Spread the top and sides of the cake with the apricot jam. If you
are using bought cakes, secure them together with a little of the
jam to make a deep, square cake. Place the cake on the platter or
cake stand.

2 Dust your work surface with icing sugar and knead the icing
to soften it slightly. Roll out 200 g (7 oz) to an 18 cm (7 inch)
square, and lay it on top of the cake. Reserve 250 g (9 oz) of
the remaining icing and roll out the remainder to a rectangle,
30 x 20 cm (12 x 8 inches). From this cut out 4 rectangles, each
18 cm (7 inches) long and 1 cm (½ inch) deeper than the cake.
Make sure that all 4 rectangles are the same length and depth.
Secure a rectangle to each cake side, pinching them gently
together at the corners to secure.

3 Dampen the top and sides of the cake board with water. Roll
out the remaining icing to a 23 cm (9 inch) square and use
it to cover the board, folding the icing down the sides and pinching
it together at the corners. Trim off the excess around the base and
at the corners.

4 Scatter the sugared almonds into the top of the cake and
carefully balance the icing-covered 'lid' in position. Cut the
ribbon into 4 even lengths. Using the tip of a knife ease one end
of each length under each side of the cake. Bring the loose ends
up over the top of the cake and fasten them together in a loose
bow. Scatter the base with the wedding confetti.

Fruit and flowers

serves 24
decoration time 30 minutes

25 cm (10 inch) round bought or homemade Rich Fruit Cake, covered with almond paste (see pages 14 and 23 for recipe and technique)

30 cm (12 inch) round white or red plate

icing sugar, for dusting

1 kg (2 lb) white ready-to-roll icing

500 g (1 lb) red fruits (e.g., strawberries, blackberries, clusters of red grapes, raspberries)

3 large open red roses

1.5 metres (5 feet) red ribbon, about 4 cm (1½ inches) wide

1 Place the cake on the plate. Dust your work surface with icing sugar and roll out the icing to a circle, 38 cm (15 inches) across. Lay it over the cake, smooth the icing around the sides and trim off the excess around the base.

2 Pile the fruits up on top of the cake, starting with the larger ones and clusters of grapes.

3 Tuck the roses in among the fruits. Secure the ribbon around the sides of the cake, finishing with a bow if liked. Using a fine tea strainer, dust the fruit and flowers with icing sugar.

tips

One of the easiest and most effective cakes to decorate, this idea is perfect for a novice to cake decorating to practise their skills.

It's ideal for a wedding anniversary, particularly a ruby wedding.

The cake can be iced a couple of weeks in advance and the fruits and flowers added at the last minute. Make sure the fruits are thoroughly dry before you place them on the icing otherwise the juices will make the icing soften and the sugar dusting will dissolve.

Red heart cake

serves 50–55
decoration time 1 hour

1 Put the larger cake on the board. Dust your work surface with icing sugar and roll out 1 kg (2 lb) of the icing to a 35 cm (14 inch) square. Lift the icing over the cake, smooth the icing down the sides and trim off the excess around the base.

2 Use the remaining icing to cover the smaller cake. Position it over the larger cake, about 2 cm (¾ inch) from one edge. Reserve the icing trimmings.

3 While the icing is still soft, gently press the cutters into the surface so they leave an impression when lifted away. If the cutters start to stick to the icing, dip them in a little icing sugar before impressing each shape. Cover the edges of the cake board with the icing trimmings.

4 Secure the ribbon around the cakes, finishing the top tier with a bow. Secure more ribbon around the cake board. Fill the glass bowl with chocolates and put it on top of the cake. Scatter more chocolates over both tiers.

12 cm (5 inch) and 23 cm (9 inch) square bought or homemade Rich Fruit Cakes, covered with almond paste (see pages 14 and 23 for recipe and technique)

28 cm (11 inch) square cake board

icing sugar, for dusting

1.5 kg (3 lb) white ready-to-roll icing

heart-shaped cookie cutters in 2 or 3 sizes

2 metres (6 feet) red ribbon, about 4 cm (1¾ inches) wide

small glass dish, about 5 cm (2 inches) in diameter

15–20 red foil-wrapped, heart-shaped chocolates

red ribbon for edges of cake board

tip

This cake is perfect for an unconventional wedding or a Valentine's Day party.
You can use Madeira cake instead of rich fruit cake – if you do, omit the layer of almond paste.

Silver wedding cake

serves 40
decoration time 1½ hours

25 cm (10 inch) round bought or
    homemade Rich Fruit Cake, covered with
    almond paste (see pages 14 and 23 for
    recipe and technique)

35 cm (14 inch) round cake board

icing sugar, for dusting

1.25 kg (2½ lb) white ready-to-roll icing

small 2 and 5 cutters

2 sheets or 1 small tub edible silver leaf

5 silver or white candles

1.5 metres (5 feet) coloured ribbon, about
    4 cm (1½ inches) wide

about 15 silver sugared almonds

white ribbon for edge of cake board

tip

Although silver leaf might seem difficult to
use at first, you'll quickly get used to it after
applying a few pieces. Because it's almost
weightless, make sure you work in a
draught-free area so that it doesn't blow
away before you've had a chance to
secure it to the cake!

1 Place the cake on the board. Reserve 200 g (7 oz) of the
icing. Dust your work surface with icing sugar and roll out the
remainder of the icing to a circle, 38 cm (15 inches) across. Lift
the icing over the cake and smooth it around the sides, trimming
off the excess around the base. Use the reserved icing to cover
the cake board, trimming off the excess around the edges.

2 Thinly roll out the icing trimmings and cut out 3 each of the
numbers 2 and 5. Set aside on a sheet of greaseproof paper.

3 Use a pair of tweezers to tear a little silver leaf from the sheet or
tub. Hold it over the cake, about 5 cm (2 inches) away from the
edge. Lightly dampen the surface of the cake where the silver is to
be applied and then lower it into position, smoothing it down with
a dry brush.

4 Arrange 3 number 25s on the cake, spacing them evenly apart
and each about 5 cm (2 inches) from the edge, and fill up the
areas between them with additional silver leaf. Apply more areas
of silver leaf to the cake board.

5 Position the candles on top of the cake and secure the ribbon
around the sides, finishing in a bow. Secure the white ribbon to
the edge of the board. Scatter the sugared almonds in clusters over
the cake and board.

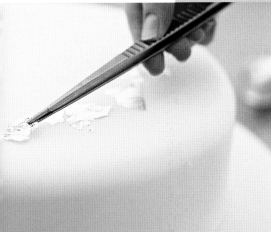

Golden wedding cake

serves 40
decoration time 1 hour

25 cm (10 inch) round bought or
    homemade Rich Fruit Cake (see page 14)

18 cm (7 inch) round cake board

4 tablespoons smooth apricot jam

icing sugar, for dusting

2 kg (4 lb) almond paste

30 cm (12 inch) round cake stand or
    glass platter

2 kg (4 lb) white ready-to-roll icing

10 gold-coloured roses

plain glass tumbler, about 15 cm
    (6 inches) tall and at least 8 cm
    (3¼ inches) in diameter

2.5 metres (8 feet) gold ribbon, 3–4 cm
    (1¼–1½ inches) wide

tip

To remove the centre of the cake, invert
a dish with a diameter of 12 cm (5 inches)
on the centre of the cake. Holding a knife
vertically, cut out the centre of the fruit
cake. Carefully remove the centre.

1 To remove cake centre, see tip. Place the removed centre on
the cake board. Brush the top and sides of both cakes with jam.

2 Measure the inner circumference of the ring cake with string.
Dust your work surface with icing sugar and roll out a little of
the almond paste. Trim it to a strip, the length of the string and
depth of the cake. Roll up the strip and unroll it in the centre of
the cake pressing it firmly in position.

3 Reserve 400 g (13 oz) of the almond paste. Roll out the
remainder to a circle, 38 cm (15 inches) across, and cut out a
circle in the centre using the small dish as a template. Lift the paste
over the cake so that the cut-out centre lines up with the hole in the
cake. Fit the paste around the sides and trim off the excess around
the base. Transfer the cake to the cake stand or platter.

4 Lightly knead the trimmings into the remaining paste and roll to
a circle, 25 cm (10 inches) across. Lay the paste over the small
cake, easing it to fit around the sides. Trim off the excess.

5 Use the white icing to cover both cakes using the same
technique as for the almond paste.

6 Secure the gold ribbon around the cakes, finishing with a
bow on the bottom tier. Pour a little water into the tumbler
and arrange several of the roses in it, cutting the stems to varying
heights. Place inside the ring cake. Use rose petals and more roses
to decorate the tops of both cakes. Position the small cake over
the glass tumbler.

Seasonal treats

Be my Valentine

serves 6–8
decoration time 30 minutes plus chilling

1 Cut the cake in half horizontally and sandwich it with a little of the ganache. Place it on the plate and spread the top and sides with the remaining ganache, swirling it in an even layer with a small palette knife.

2 Measure the circumference of the cake with a piece of string. Cut a strip of greaseproof paper 2 cm (¾ inch) longer than the string and 5 cm (2 inches) deeper than the cake.

3 Break the chocolate into pieces and melt them in a bowl set over a pan of gently simmering water. Spoon half the chocolate on to the strip of greaseproof paper. Spread it to the edge of one long side and to 1 cm (½ inch) from both short ends. On the other long side of the strip use a thick paintbrush or pastry brush to spread the chocolate to the edges in an uneven, jagged line. Return the chocolate in the bowl to the pan, but turn off the heat so the remaining chocolate stays melted over the warm water.

4 Leave the chocolate strip to cool slightly, but do not allow it to set. Then carefully wrap it around the cake (paper side outwards) so that the jagged edge is uppermost. Chill for about 30 minutes until the chocolate is brittle.

5 Meanwhile, spoon 2 tablespoons of the remaining chocolate into a small bowl and beat in a dot of food colouring paste. Turn it into a paper piping bag and snip off the tip. Pipe about 12 heart shapes on to a sheet of greaseproof paper. Use a small teaspoon to fill the centre of each heart with the remaining chocolate, nudging it gently to the edges. Chill for 30 minutes.

6 Carefully peel away the paper from the cake. Once the chocolate hearts have set, peel away the paper and arrange the hearts on top of the cake. Scatter with the heart sweets.

12–15 cm (5–6 inch) round bought or homemade Rich Chocolate Cake (see page 13)

single quantity White Chocolate Ganache (see page 18)

pink, lilac or cream-coloured plate

200 g (7 oz) white chocolate

pink or lilac food colouring paste

handful of small heart-shaped candies

tip
Make sure you use food colouring paste for the decoration because liquid colour will make the chocolate solidify.

Mother's day

serves 12
decoration time 45 minutes

1 egg white

75 g (3 oz) caster sugar

about 25 red, pink and yellow primroses

18 cm (7 inch) round bought or homemade
    Madeira Cake (see page 11)

150 g (5 oz) lemon curd

20 cm (8 inch) round or square cream plate

double quantity Buttercream (see page 16)

tip

Frosted flowers keep well for several weeks
if stored in an airtight container. Make sure
they're completely dry first, then arrange
them in layers, interleaving each with
kitchen paper.

1 Lightly whisk the egg white in a small bowl with 1 tablespoon of water until it is broken up. Put the sugar in a separate bowl. Gently pull one of the flowers away from its calyx. Using a paintbrush or your fingers lightly coat each side of the petals in egg white. Sprinkle with caster sugar until completely coated. Transfer the flower, face down, to a sheet of baking parchment or greaseproof paper. If the flower starts to fall flat, losing its shape, support it on a tiny crumpled ball of greaseproof paper. Frost the remaining flowers in the same way and leave them to dry for at least 1 hour or overnight.

2 Cut the cake horizontally into 3 and sandwich the layers together with lemon curd. Place the cake on the plate.

3 Spread a thin layer of buttercream over the top and sides of the cake to seal in the crumbs. Spread the remaining buttercream over the cake, smoothing it out with a palette knife. Arrange the frosted flowers around the top edges of the cake.

Chocolate egg cake

serves 10
decoration time 30 minutes

100 g (3½ oz) milk chocolate

200 g (7 oz) plain chocolate

150 ml (¼ pint) double cream

18 cm (7 inch) bought or homemade
   Rich Chocolate Cake (see page 13)

23–25 cm (9–10 inch) round flat plate

selection of plain, milk or white chocolate
   eggs

tip

If the cream boils in the pan, remove it from
the heat and let it cool a little before you
add the chocolate. It'll take a little longer
to thicken so that it can be spread over the
cake, so keep an eye on it as it cools.

1 Break the chocolate into pieces and melt them in a bowl set over a pan of gently simmering water. Line a baking sheet with baking parchment or greaseproof paper. Using a teaspoon scribble the melted chocolate in irregular lines all over the paper. Don't try to be neat – the more casual the lines are, the better they'll be. Put the chocolate in the refrigerator for 20 minutes.

2 Chop the plain chocolate. Heat 100 ml (3½ fl oz) of the cream in a small heavy-based saucepan until it is bubbling around the edges but not boiling. Remove from the heat and stir in the chocolate. Turn the mixture into a bowl and stir until it is melted and smooth. Stir in the remaining cream.

3 Cut the cake in half horizontally and sandwich it with a little of the chocolate cream. Put it on the plate and tip the remaining chocolate cream over the top, spreading it with a palette knife so it covers the sides in swirls.

4 Take the milk chocolate shapes from the refrigerator and peel away the parchment or greaseproof paper. Break the chocolate into long, irregular pieces. Scatter them over the cake and pile the eggs on top. Keep the cake in a cool place until ready to serve.

Easter egg

serves 8–10
Preparation and cooking time about 1½ hours
decoration time 30 minutes

1 Grease a 2.5 litre (4 pint) ovenproof basin and line the base with a circle of greaseproof paper. Turn the cake mixture into the basin and level the surface. Bake in a preheated oven, 180°C (350°F), Gas Mark 4, for 1–1¼ hours or until the cake feels just firm in the centre. Leave to cool in the basin. Run a knife around the edges of the basin and invert the cake on a board. To make the egg shape, start by cutting a vertical slice, 5 cm (2 inches) wide, off 2 opposite sides of the cake. Keeping the knife vertical, cut away more of the cake at one end to make a pointed egg shape, then round off all the edges of the cake, remembering that the cake will be shallower at the pointed end than at the thick end. Keep the trimmings. Slice the egg shape vertically into 3 layers and sandwich them together with a little of the chocolate spread. Cover the egg with the remaining chocolate spread.

2 Dust your work surface with icing sugar and roll out the icing to an oval, 33 x 28 cm (13 x 11 inches). Lift the icing over the cake and smooth it to fit around the sides. Trim off the excess around the base. Transfer the cake to a tray or board lined with baking parchment or greaseproof paper.

3 Break the chocolate into pieces and put them in a bowl over a pan of gently simmering water until the chocolate has melted. Put the chocolate in a paper piping bag and snip off the tip. Using a scribbling action, pipe lines of chocolate diagonally across the chocolate egg. Using a fish slice, carefully transfer the cake to the serving plate and keep it in a cool place until the chocolate has set.

4 Use the tip of a knife to tuck one end of the ribbon under the end of the egg. Wrap the ribbon down the length of the egg and tuck it under the other end. Use the remaining ribbon to make a large bow for the top. Secure in position with a little tape.

3-egg quantity Rich Chocolate Cake (see page 13)

300 g (10 oz) chocolate hazelnut spread

icing sugar, for dusting

500 g (1 lb) chocolate brown ready-to-roll icing

50 g (2 oz) milk chocolate

oval plate, about 28 cm (11 inches) long

1.5 metres (5 feet) ribbon, about 4 cm (1½ inches) wide

tips

This is a perfect cake for an Easter centrepiece, as long as you're confident about shaping the sponge cake into an egg shape. Once the cake is decorated it will keep well in a cool place for several days.

There are quite a lot of trimmings from this cake, so keep them for a chocolate trifle or mix them with melted chocolate to make truffle cakes.

Easter cupcakes

makes 12
decoration time 30 minutes

75 g (3 oz) milk chocolate

75 g (3 oz) plain chocolate

single quantity Chocolate Fudge Icing
(see page 19)

12 bought or homemade Vanilla Cupcakes
(see page 12)

36 mini-chocolate eggs

large round or square plate

1 Use a vegetable peeler to pare thick curls from both the milk and plain chocolate. If the chocolate breaks off in brittle shards, it's too cold, so pop it in the microwave for 10 seconds and try again. You might need to microwave the chocolate several times before it's soft enough, but take care that it doesn't melt.

2 Spread the chocolate fudge icing over the cupcakes, scattering each one as you go with plenty of the chocolate curls.

3 Arrange 3 mini-chocolate eggs in the centre of each cake and pile up the cakes on the plate.

tips

You might want to make a double batch of cupcakes, depending on how many hungry visitors you'll see during the Easter holiday.

Use chocolate from a chunky chocolate bar for the curls so that they are as large as possible. For a finishing touch, try tying some fine ribbon around some of the cupcakes. You will find this is easier if you do it before you add the icing.

Pumpkin patch

serves 24
decoration time 45 minutes

20 cm (8 inch) round bought or homemade
   Madeira Cake (see page 11)

6 tablespoons apricot jam

double quantity Buttercream (see page 16)

30–35 cm (12–14 inch) round wooden
   board

250 g (8 oz) orange ready-to-roll icing

icing sugar, for dusting

15 g (½ oz) chocolate brown ready-to-roll
   icing

8 sprigs artificial foliage, each containing
   3–5 leaves

tip

The little pumpkins on this cake are
surprisingly easy to make and look stunning
nestling in their green leaves. They'll look
even more effective if they're all different
sizes, so don't be too precise.

1 Cut the cake in half horizontally and sandwich it together with
the jam and a little of the buttercream. Place the cake on the
board and spread the remaining buttercream in an even layer over
the top and sides, swirling it decoratively with a palette knife.

2 Roll the orange icing between the palms of your hands into
balls of varying sizes, dusting your hands with icing sugar if the
icing starts to stick. Flatten each ball slightly into a pumpkin shape
and make deep grooves evenly all around the sides with the back
of a knife.

3 Roll the brown icing into a rope and cut it into short lengths.
Dampen one end of each length with a paintbrush and secure
them to the pumpkins for the stalks.

4 Arrange some of the foliage on top of the cake, nestling all but
one of the pumpkins among the leaves. Arrange more leaves
and the remaining pumpkin around the base of the cake.

Spider's web

serves 16
decoration time 30 minutes

20 cm (8 inch) round bought or homemade
  Madeira Cake (see page 11)

double quantity Buttercream (see page 16)

33–35 cm (13–14 inch) round plate,
  preferably red or orange

icing sugar, for dusting

1 kg (2 lb) white ready-to-roll icing

1 tube black writing icing

black food colouring

15 g (½ oz) black ready-to-roll icing

1 flat liquorice bootlace

several sweet snakes or insects

orange or black candles

tip

Using a tube of icing to create the web
is much easier than it looks, but there's
enough icing in the tube to pipe a web
on a plate if you want to practise first.

1 Cut the cake in half horizontally and sandwich it together with half the buttercream. Put it on the plate and spread over the remaining buttercream.

2 Dust your work surface with icing sugar and roll out about 875 g (1¾ lb) of the white icing to a circle, 33 cm (13 inches) across. Lay the icing over the cake and smooth it around the sides, trimming off the excess icing around the base.

3 Use the tube of black writing icing to pipe 6 lines over the top of the cake, crossing them in the centre. Working from the centre outwards, pipe curved lines of icing to resemble a spider's web.

4 Roll 50 g (2 oz) of the reserved white icing into a ball, then mould it into a ghost shape. Press the shape on to the surface to make sure it stands upright, then secure it to one side of the web with a dampened paintbrush. Paint the ghost's eyes and mouth with the black food colouring and a fine brush.

5 To make the spider, roll the black icing into a ball and put it on the web. Cut 8 pieces of liquorice, each 4 cm (1½ inches) long, and secure 4 on either side of the black icing ball. Arrange a few sweet snakes or insects on the web.

6 Roll the remaining white icing into a long, thin rope and arrange in a curvy line around the sides of the cake. Push the candles into the icing for support.

Snowy cupcakes

makes 12
decoration time 20 minutes plus drying

200 g (7 oz) icing sugar and extra for
   dusting

50 g (2 oz) white ready-to-roll icing

3 cm (1¼ inch) star cutter

2 tablespoons lemon juice

12 bought or homemade Vanilla Cupcakes
   (see page 12)

50 g (2 oz) desiccated coconut

tip

These little cakes make a lovely gift,
particularly if you put them in a shallow,
square box, tied with a stunning ribbon.

   They couldn't be easier to decorate and
are best made up to a day in advance so
they're perfectly fresh when you present
them to your guests.

1 Dust your work surface with icing sugar and roll out the icing.
Cut out 12 small stars. Transfer them to a baking sheet lined with
baking parchment or greaseproof paper and leave them to harden
for at least 1 hour.

2 Beat the icing sugar in a bowl with 1 tablespoon lemon juice.
Gradually add the remaining juice until the icing just holds its
shape but is not too thick to spread. You might not need all the
lemon juice.

3 Use a small palette knife to spread the icing over the cupcakes.
Sprinkle plenty of coconut over each cupcake and gently press
a star shape into the top.

Christmas star

serves 12
decoration time about 1 hour plus drying

icing sugar, for dusting

1.25 kg (2½ lb) white ready-to-roll icing

5 cm (2 inch) and 3 cm (1¼ inch) star cutters

25 cm (10 inch) round bought or
homemade Madeira Cake (see page 11)

double quantity Buttercream (see page 16)

4 tablespoons smooth raspberry or
strawberry jam

28 cm (11 inch) round cake board

selection of silver and gold balls

silver or gold food colouring

ribbon for edge of cake board

tips

Freeze the sponge trimmings from the
cake and use them in a Christmas trifle.
To make shaping easier, you might
even be able to buy, or hire, a star-shaped
cake cutter, in which case you might prefer
to use a rich fruit cake mixture instead of
a Madeira cake.

1 Dust your work surface with icing sugar and thinly roll out 100 g (3½ oz) of the icing. Use the larger cutter to cut out plenty of star shapes. Cut out the centre of each star with the small cutter and transfer the stars to a lined baking sheet. Leave for several hours or overnight to harden.

2 Cut out a circle of paper, 25 cm (10 inches) across, and fold it in half. Fold the halved paper into 3 to make a wedge 6 sheets thick. Make a pencil mark 5 cm (2 inches) from the point and an equal distance from the sides. Draw a line from each outer corner to the pencil mark. Cut along the lines and open out the paper into a star. Rest the star over the cake and use it as a template for cutting out a star shape. Cut the cake in half horizontally and sandwich with half the buttercream and all the jam. Spread the remaining buttercream over the top and sides of the cake.

4 Thinly roll out a further 275 g (9 oz) of the icing and use it to cover the cake board, trimming off and reserving the excess around the base. Lift the cake on to the board. Roll out half the remaining icing and cut out long strips, each the depth of the cake. Use these to cover the sides of the cake, pushing the strips well into the corners and emphasizing the star shape by pinching the icing into points. Work in manageable strips of icing.

6 Roll out the remaining icing to a circle, 25 cm (10 inches) across, and use the paper template to cut out a star. Dampen the top edges of the icing around the sides and lift the star into position on the cake, pressing the icing together around the edges.

7 Press the silver and gold balls into the top and sides of the cake and over the board. If necessary, dampen the icing with a fine brush to help them stick. Paint the star shapes and arrange them on the cake. Secure the ribbon around the edge of the cake board.

Jagged jewel cake

serves 24
decoration time 20 minutes

20 cm (8 inch) round bought or homemade
Rich Fruit Cake, covered with almond
paste (see pages 14 and 23 for recipe
and technique)

25–30 cm (10–12 inch) round glass plate,
preferably red

icing sugar for dusting

1 kg (2 lb) white ready-to-roll icing

200 g (7 oz) red, purple, orange and green
clear boiled sweets

6 red tea lights

1 metre (39 inches) red ribbon, about 4 cm
(1½ inches) wide

tip

The sweets can be melted up to 2 days
in advance. Once they have cooled, leave
them on the foil-lined baking sheet and
cover tightly with lightly oiled clingfilm. This
will stop the sweets softening and turning
sticky. Once they are on the cake, the
sweets should stay brittle for a couple of
days before they begin to soften.

1 Put the cake on the plate. Dust your work surface with icing sugar
and roll out the icing to a circle, 33 cm (13 inches) across. Lay it
over the cake, smoothing the icing around the sides and trimming
off the excess around the base.

2 Line a large baking sheet with kitchen foil. Unwrap the
sweets and space them about 4 cm (1½ inches) apart on the
foil, making sure the colours are evenly mixed. Put the sweets in
a preheated oven, 200°C (400°F), Gas Mark 6, for 3–5 minutes
until the sweets have melted together and are bubbling but
not turning brown. Watch closely for the last couple of minutes
because the sweets will quickly darken and start to burn. Leave
them to cool on the foil.

3 Peel away the foil from the sweets and use your fingers to break
the sweets into large, jagged pieces.

4 Arrange the tea lights in a circle in the centre of the cake.
Surround these with the sweet brittle, pushing the pieces gently
into the icing. Tie the ribbon around the cake and light the candles
just before serving.

Candle garland

serves 40
decoration time 30 minutes

25 cm (10 inch) round bought or
  homemade Rich Fruit Cake, covered with
  almond paste (see pages 14 and 23 for
  recipe and technique)

30 cm (12 inch) round glass platter

double quantity Royal Icing (see page 19)

5 small clementines

5 tea lights

several small sprigs of bay leaves

5 cinnamon sticks

12 gold dragees

1–1.5 metres (39–58½ inches) gold-edged
  ribbon, about 3 cm (1¼ inches) wide

1 Put the cake on the platter. Cover it with the icing, swirling it over the top and sides with a palette knife.

2 Cut a slice off the top of each clementine and scoop out as much flesh as possible. Dry the clementine skins on kitchen paper. The flesh sometimes comes away cleanly, leaving dry skins, in which case you won't need to dry them.

3 Place a tea light inside each clementine and arrange them around the top of the cake. Tuck the sprigs of bay leaves, the cinnamon sticks and dragees between the fruits.

4 Tie the ribbon around the sides of the cake, finishing with a bow if liked.

tip

You can cover a cake with royal icing up to 2 weeks in advance, but leave the clementines and other decoration until the day before you want to serve the cake so that they don't deteriorate.

Glacé fruit cake

serves 24
decoration time 30 minutes

20 cm (8 inch) round bought or homemade Rich Fruit Cake (see page 14)

100 g (3½ oz) smooth apricot jam

3 tablespoons brandy

icing sugar, for dusting

500 g (1 lb) yellow or white almond paste

25 cm (10 inch) round serving plate

250 g (8 oz) selection of crystallized fruits (e.g., cherries, papaya, mango, melon, pineapple)

4–5 dates, halved and pitted

1–1.5 metres (39–58½ inches) orange ribbon, 5 cm (2 inches) wide

tip

This cake is a perfect choice for marzipan lovers or those who find icing just too sweet. You can buy mixed bags of glacé fruits, including pineapple, papaya and mango, to which you can add some glacé cherries. Boxes of whole glacé fruits are also available – although they are rather expensive – from delicatessens and department stores. These can be cut into large pieces so that the shape of the fruit is still recognizable.

1 Put the cake on a baking sheet. Blend the jam with the brandy and spread a little over the sides of the cake.

2 Measure the circumference of the cake with a piece of string. Dust your work surface with icing sugar and roll out three-quarters of the almond paste to a strip the length of the string and 1 cm (½ inch) deeper than the cake. Secure the strip around the cake.

3 Halve the remaining almond paste and roll out each half to a long, thin rope, slightly shorter than the string. Twist the 2 ropes together and arrange the twist around the top edges of the cake. Place the cake under a moderate grill for 2–3 minutes, watching the paste closely until it is evenly toasted. (Rotate the baking sheet slightly to get an even colour.)

4 Transfer the cake to a serving plate. Cut all the fruits into equal pieces. Brush the top of the cake with a little more glaze and scatter over the fruits. Brush the fruits with the remaining glaze and secure the ribbon around the sides.

Box of toys

serves 24
decoration time 30 minutes

18 cm (7 inch) square bought or homemade
  Rich Fruit Cake, covered with almond
  paste (see pages 14 and 23 for recipe
  and technique)

25 cm (10 inch) square plate or cake board

icing sugar, for dusting

500 g (1 lb) white ready-to-roll icing

250 g (8 oz) deep green ready-to-roll icing

25 g (1 oz) red ready-to-roll icing

selection of small wooden or plastic toys
  for decoration

1 tube green or red writing icing

1 metre (39 inches) fine red ribbon

1 Put the cake on the plate or board. Dust your work surface with icing sugar and roll out the white icing to a 30 cm (12 inch) square. Lay it over the cake, smoothing the icing around the sides and trimming off the excess around the base.

2 Thinly roll out the green icing to a 23 cm (9 inch) square. Use a sharp knife to trim off the edges in deep scallops.

3 Lightly brush the top of the cake with a dampened paintbrush and lay the green icing over the cake so that the scalloped edges fall around the sides.

4 Roll the red icing into small balls and secure one to the tip of each scallop. Arrange the small toys on top of the cake, securing them with dots of icing from the tube. Tie the ribbon around the base.

tip

The best place to buy little toys for decorating this cake is a toy shop with a good selection of tiny 'stocking fillers'. Add to these a few small cake decorations – Santas and snowmen – and you'll quickly accumulate a colourful collection. Remove them all from the cake before cutting.

Party time

Happy birthday cupcakes

makes 24 small cupcakes
decoration time about 1 hour

18 cm (7 inch) bought or homemade square
 Madeira Cake (see page 11)

24 paper cake cases

large rectangular board or tray

1 egg white

2 tablespoons lemon juice

500 g (1 lb) icing sugar

pink food colouring

silver balls

6 small sugar flowers

pink or white candles, optional

tip

When you're blending icing sugar with
water or lemon juice, take care not to add
too much liquid or the icing will be too thin.
Just a few drops will make a big difference
to the consistency of the icing.

1 Cut any excess dome off the top of the cake. Cut the cake horizontally in half. From each half cut out 12 rectangles, each 4 cm (1¾ inches) long, and arrange them in paper cases in a rectangle on the board or tray.

2 Beat the egg white and lemon juice in a bowl with a little of the icing sugar. Gradually blend in the remainder to make a paste that just holds its shape. Turn half the mixture into a separate bowl and colour it pale pink. Spoon about 2 tablespoons of each colour into separate paper piping bags and snip off the tips so that the icing can be piped in a thick line.

3 Thin the remaining pink and white icing with a dash of water or extra lemon juice until each thickly coats the back of the spoon. Spoon each icing over the tops of half the cupcakes.

4 Use the icing in the bags, the silver balls and sugar flowers to decorate the tops of the cakes as illustrated, writing a name, a message or an age if liked. Arrange candles around the edges of the cakes, if used, and store in a cool place for up to 24 hours.

Big birthday

serves 45–50
decoration time 1 hour

15 cm (6 inch), 20 cm (8 inch) and 25 cm (10 inch) round bought or homemade Madeira Cakes (see page 11) or Rich Chocolate Cakes (see page 13)

quadruple quantity Buttercream (see page 16) or triple quantity White Chocolate Ganache (see page 18)

30 cm (12 inch) plate

icing sugar, for dusting

200 g (7 oz) deep red ready-to-roll icing

200 g (7 oz) dark blue ready-to-roll icing

200 g (7 oz) purple ready-to-roll icing

1 tube of red or blue writing icing

number birthday candles (e.g., 18 or 21)

fine blue and purple parcel ribbon

1 Place the largest cake on the plate and spread it with a scant half of the buttercream or ganache, smoothing it in an even layer with a palette knife.

2 Put the medium-sized cake on top and spread it with more buttercream or ganache in the same way. Position the smallest cake on top and spread it evenly with the remaining buttercream or ganache.

3 Dust your work surface with icing sugar and shape the coloured icings into little parcel shapes. Use the writing icing to pipe ribbons on the parcels.

4 Position the candles on top of the cake, then drape lengths of ribbon over the top and down the sides of the cake. Tuck the parcels in among the ribbons.

tips

Celebratory candles are available in all numbers, so this is a quick and easy celebration cake for any important birthday. Cover the cake with buttercream or ganache a day in advance and keep it in a cool place.

It can also be decorated with ready-to-roll icing. You will need about 2 kg (4 lb). Cover each cake separately with icing before stacking them on the plate.

50th birthday

serves 30
preparation and cooking time about 1 hour
decoration time 1 hour

1 Grease and line the number tins and place them on a large baking sheet. Divide the cake mixture between the tins and level the surface. Bake in a preheated oven, 160°C (325°F), Gas Mark 3, for about 50 minutes or until just firm and a skewer, inserted into the centres, comes out clean. Leave to cool.

2 Cut the cakes in half horizontally and sandwich them with the buttercream and half the jam. Spread the remaining jam over the tops and sides of the cakes.

3 Dust your work surface with icing sugar and roll out 500 g (1 lb) of the pale blue icing very thinly to a rectangle that is slightly smaller than the cake board. Dampen the board and lift the icing on to the board. Smooth it down gently with the palms of your hands and trim the icing, leaving a border 2 cm (¾ inch) wide around the edges.

4 Thinly roll out 200 g (7 oz) of the brown icing and cut out long strips. Use these to cover the edges of the board, trimming off the excess around the edges. Reserve the trimmings.

5 Roll out half the dark blue icing and use it to cover one of the numbers, easing the icing down the sides and trimming off the excess around the base. If necessary patch up any gaps around the sides. Carefully transfer the cake to the board. Cover the second cake with the remaining icing and put it on the board.

6 Roll the remaining pale blue and brown icing into long, thin ropes. Twist together and cut into manageable lengths. Drape over the cakes, securing with a dampened paintbrush. Arrange the tea lights around the numbers and secure the brown ribbon around the sides of the board.

large 5 and 0 number cake tins

2 x 5-egg quantity Madeira Cake mixture (see page 11)

double quantity Buttercream (see page 16)

8 tablespoons smooth raspberry or strawberry jam

icing sugar, for dusting

750 g (1½ lb) pale blue ready-to-roll icing

300 g (10 oz) chocolate brown ready-to-roll icing

45 x 35 cm (18 x 14 inches) rectangular cake board

1 kg (2 lb) dark blue ready-to-roll icing

8–10 tea lights

2 metres (6 feet) brown ribbon for edges of cake board

tips

This makes a great cake for a large party of adults. It cuts into plenty of portions, is not too difficult to ice and works well for any age. Large number tins can be hired for a couple of days for making the cake.

It's easier to ice the centres of numbers such as 0, 6, 8 and 9 with a strip of icing before you cover the rest of the cake.

Summer celebration cake

serves 28
decoration time 45 minutes plus chilling

15 cm (6 inch) and 20 cm (8 inch) round bought or homemade Rich Chocolate Cakes (see page 13)

25 cm (10 inch) round platter

double quantity White Chocolate Ganache (see page 18)

375 g (12 oz) white chocolate

500g (1 lb) soft fruits (e.g., strawberries, raspberries, blueberries and redcurrants)

100 g (3½ oz) redcurrant jelly

tips

For an even more intense chocolatey experience, make up an extra quantity of chocolate ganache and use it to sandwich the cakes together in 3 layers.

An extra pair of hands will make the job of wrapping the collar around the larger cake easier.

1 Put the larger cake on the platter. Use a palette knife to spread two-thirds of the ganache over the top and sides. Position the smaller cake on top and cover it with the remaining ganache.

2 Break the chocolate into small pieces and put them in a bowl over a pan of gently simmering water. Leave until the chocolate has melted. Use a piece of string to measure the circumferences of both cakes. Cut 2 strips of greaseproof paper, each 2.5 cm (1 inch) longer than the circumference of the cakes and 2 cm (¾ inch) deeper.

3 Spread the melted chocolate over each strip of paper to within 1 cm (½ inch) of the ends and almost to the edges. Leave for 1–2 minutes until the chocolate has cooled slightly (but not started to set), then wrap the short strip around the small cake and the longer strip around the larger cake, paper side out.

4 Chill the cakes for about 30–60 minutes or until the chocolate is brittle, then carefully peel away the paper. Pile the fruits over the top of each cake, letting the redcurrant sprigs spill slightly over the sides.

5 To glaze the fruits, melt the redcurrant jelly with 1 tablespoon water until smooth. Use a pastry brush to coat the fruits evenly with the mixture.

Summer carnival

serves 16
decoration time 1 hour

1 Slice the domed surface off each cake and cut the cakes in half horizontally. Use half the buttercream to sandwich the cakes together. Place one cake on top of the other, sandwiching with a little more buttercream. Use a sharp knife cut a 'waist' out of the stacked cakes so that the stack is wider at the top and base. Place the cake on the board and cover it with the remaining buttercream.

2 Measure the circumference at the base of the cake with a piece of string. Dust your work surface with icing sugar and roll out 250 g (8 oz) of the yellow icing to a strip the length of the string and half the overall depth of the cake. Wrap the icing around the cake, easing it to fit where the cake is narrower in the centre. Roll out 250 g (8 oz) of the red icing and use it to cover the top half of the cake.

3 Thinly roll out the orange icing and cut it into strips, each 3 cm (1¼ inches) wide. Make diagonal cuts across the strips to create large diamond shapes. Secure around the centre of the cake using a dampened paintbrush and add halved diamond shapes around the cake base.

4 Roll out the remaining yellow icing and cut out plenty of small yellow circles with the cutter. Secure these to the cake, then arrange more circles on the plate. Using the red icing trimmings, roll out a circle, 15 cm (6 inches) across and use to cover the top. Pile plenty of steamers or ribbons and party poppers or tooters on top of the cake.

2 x 15 cm (6 inch) round bought or homemade Madeira Cakes (see page 11)

double quantity Buttercream (see page 16)

28–30 cm (11–12 inch) round, brightly coloured plate

icing sugar, for dusting

300 g (10 oz) yellow ready-to-roll icing

300 g (10 oz) red ready-to-roll icing

200 g (7 oz) orange ready-to-roll icing

2 cm (¾ inch) round cutter

selection of brightly coloured streamers or ribbons and party poppers or tooters

tips

If you can't get orange icing you can make it by kneading red and yellow ready-to-roll icing together.

Buy large bags of party poppers and streamers from party and catering stores.

Triple chocolate croquembouche

serves 10–12
preparation and cooking time 40 minutes
decoration time 30 minutes

40 choux pastry buns (see page 15)

double quantity White Chocolate Ganache
(see page 18)

flat plate, at least 28 cm (11 inches) across

200 g (7 oz) plain chocolate

200 g (7 oz) milk chocolate

12–15 gold-coloured chocolate dragees,
roughly chopped

1 When the choux pastry buns are cool, fill each one with a
heaped teaspoonful of the white chocolate ganache.

2 Break half the plain chocolate into pieces and put them in a
bowl over a saucepan of lightly simmering water until the
chocolate has melted. Dip the base of about 10 buns in the melted
chocolate and arrange them in a circle, about 23 cm (9 inches)
across, on the serving plate. (When it sets, the chocolate will hold
the buns together.) Put about 3 buns in the centre.

3 Gradually build up layers of buns to form a cone shape,
dipping each bun in melted chocolate so that it is secured to
the buns underneath. Finish with a single bun on top.

4 Melt the remaining plain chocolate and the milk chocolate in
separate bowls and spoon over the buns. Tuck the chocolate
dragees in among the buns to finish. Keep the cake in a cool place
until ready to serve.

tips

Make the buns in advance, put them in
plastic bags and freeze them, re-crisping
them in a moderate oven for 5 minutes
before use.

If you're assembling the croquembouche
in hot weather you might need to chill it
halfway through so that it doesn't collapse.

A midsummer night's dream

serves 16
decoration time 1 hour

1 Slice any dome off the top of the cake. Cut the cake in half horizontally and sandwich it with half the buttercream and all the jam. Put it on the plate and spread with the remaining buttercream.

2 Dust your work surface with icing sugar and roll out the lilac icing to a 35 cm (14 inch) square. Lay the icing over the cake and smooth it down the sides, trimming off the excess around the base.

3 Roll out the green icing to a 23 cm (9 inch) square. Lightly brush the cake board with water and lift the icing over the board. Smooth the icing over the sides and trim off the excess around the base. Reserve the trimmings. Position the board on top of the cake.

4 Place the battery-operated lights on the centre of the board and position the flowers and foliage over and around the lights, making sure that the lights are evenly spaced among the flowers and that you're able to activate the switch. If necessary, use the icing trimmings to prop up the flowers on the board. Scatter the pebbles over the board to fill the gaps and conceal the batteries and wires.

23 cm (9 inch) square bought or homemade Madeira Cake (see page 11)

single quantity Buttercream (see page 16)

8 tablespoons raspberry or strawberry jam

28–30 cm (11–12 inch) square plate

icing sugar, for dusting

1 kg (2 lb) lilac ready-to-roll icing

250 g (8 oz) deep green ready-to-roll icing

20 cm (8 inch) square cake board

1 small set battery-operated decorative lights

small bunch wired silk foliage

small bunch pink, purple or cream-coloured wired silk flowers

small bunch lavender

about 750g (1½ lb) ornamental cream-coloured pebbles

tip

The larger the party, the bigger you can make this cake! Whatever cake size you use, the board should be 2.5 cm (1 inch) smaller to support the decoration.

Fireworks night

serves 12
preparation and cooking time about 1 hour
decoration time 1 hour plus drying

icing sugar, for dusting

100 g (3½ oz) yellow ready-to-roll icing

5 cm (2 inch) and 3 cm (1¼ inch) star cutters

200 g (7 oz) orange ready-to-roll icing

100 g (3½ oz) red ready-to-roll icing

20 lengths heavy gauge florist's wire, cut to
    various lengths

4-egg quantity Madeira Cake mixture
    (see page 11)

double quantity Buttercream (see page 16)

20 cm (8 inch) square plate

500 g (1 lb) dark blue ready-to-roll icing

tip
Before you push the wires into the top of the
cake, wrap a tiny piece of clingfilm or foil
around the end of each wire. Alternatively,
use small plastic 'flower picks', which are
available from cake decorating suppliers.

1 Dust your work surface with icing sugar and roll out three-quarters of the yellow icing. Cut out stars in both sizes. Roll out a third of the orange icing and cut out more stars. Lightly dampen some of the large yellow stars with water and secure some of the small orange stars to them. Bend the tip of a length of florist's wire over to create a hook and push it into the centre of a star. Repeat with the other stars. Cut out more shapes, such as 'wheels' of red and yellow icing and long, ribbony shapes, and thread these on to more wires. Transfer all the shapes to a large baking sheet lined with baking parchment and leave them to harden for several hours, preferably overnight. Reserve the icing trimmings.

2 Turn the cake mixture into a greased and lined square tin, 25 cm (10 inches) and level the surface. Bake in a preheated oven, 160°C (325°F), Gas Mark 3 for about 50 minutes until just firm and a skewer, inserted into the cenre, comes out clean. Leave to cool.

2 Slice the dome off the top of the cake and cut it into 4 equal pieces. Sandwich the cakes in a stack with half the buttercream and transfer to the plate. Spread the remaining buttercream over the top and sides.

3 Roll out more orange icing and cut out a 12 cm (5 inch) square. Place this on top of the cake. Roll out the blue icing and cut out 4 squares to cover the sides. Position these around the cake, pressing them together at the corners to seal. Use strips of the remaining orange icing to decorate the top and bottom edges.

4 Use the red and yellow icing trimmings to cut out ribbon and star shapes. Secure these around the box. Press the wired shapes into the top of the cake to finish.

Birthday present

serves 40
decoration time 30 minutes

23 cm (9 inch) square bought or homemade
    Rich Fruit Cake, covered with almond
    paste (see pages 14 and 23 for recipe
    and technique)

30 cm (12 inch) square cake board

1.5 kg (3 lb) white ready-to-roll icing

deep red or pink food colouring

icing sugar, for dusting

2 metres (6 feet) soft grey ribbon, about
    2.5 cm (1 inch) wide

2 metres (6 feet) pale pink ribbon, about
    5 cm (2 inches) wide

pale pink ribbon for edges of cake board

tips

The ribbons are the focal point of this
easy cake, so choose soft, delicate colours
for a romantic look, or use an alternative
colour scheme for a bolder effect.

   Instead of fruit cake you could use a
bought or homemade Madeira cake,
sandwiched with buttercream.

1 Place the cake on the board. Reserve 200 g (7 oz) of the icing
and lightly knead the remainder. Use a cocktail stick to dot the
icing very carefully and cautiously with food colouring. The more
colour you add, the more vibrant the finished result will be.

2 Roll out the icing to a thick sausage. Fold it into 3 and roll
again, repeating the process until the icing is marbled with
colour. Dust your work surface with icing sugar and roll out the
icing to a square that will cover the cake. Smooth the icing down
the sides and trim off the excess around the base.

3 Lay the narrower ribbon over the wider ribbon. Use the tip of a
knife to tuck the ends of the ribbons under the base of the cake
on one side. Bring the ribbons over to the other side and cut to fit,
tucking the ends under the cake. Repeat on the other 2 sides and
shape a generous bow for the top. Secure the bow in position with
a little clear tape.

4 Use the reserved white icing to cover the edges of the cake
board. Secure the pink ribbon around the edges of the board.

Champagne bottle

serves 15
decoration time 1 hour

icing sugar, for dusting

300g (10oz) grey ready-to-roll icing

35 x 25 cm (14 x 10 inch) rectangular cake
  board

2 bought or homemade Swiss Rolls
  (see page 12)

single quantity Buttercream (see page 16)

500 g (1 lb) dark green ready-to-roll icing

75 g (3 oz) black ready-to-roll icing

50 g (2 oz) white ready-to-roll icing

black and gold food colouring

dark green ribbon for edges of cake board

tip

If you're using a bought Swiss roll you
might need to buy an extra one and add an
additional layer because they tend to be
much thinner than homemade ones.

1 Dust your work surface with icing sugar and thinly roll out the
grey icing to a rectangle that will cover the cake board. Trim off
the excess around the base.

2 Place the Swiss rolls on the work surface, end to end, and cut
them down to an overall length of 30 cm (12 inches). Cut a
'neck' out of one end, trimming off the cut edges to make a curved
bottle shape. Use a little buttercream to sandwich the join in the
cakes, then spread a thin layer all over the cakes.

3 Roll out a little of the green icing and cut an oval, the same
diameter as the base of the bottle. Press it into position. Roll out
the remaining green icing and use it to cover the rest of the bottle,
smoothing it to fit over the neck of the bottle and trimming off the
excess around the base. Use a fish slice to transfer the cake to the
board, supporting it carefully under the join.

4 Roll out the black icing and use it to decorate the top of the
bottle. Use the white icing and the black icing trimmings to
shape the labels.

5 Decorate the bottle with the black and gold food colourings,
using a fine paintbrush. Secure the ribbon around the board.

Box of chocolates

serves 18
decoration time 30 minutes

18 cm (7 inch) square bought or homemade
  Rich Chocolate Cake (see page 13)

23 cm (9 inch) square flat plate

single quantity Dark Chocolate Ganache
  (see page 18)

4 x 100 g (3½ oz) chocolate bars, each
  19 x 9 cm (7½ x 3½ inches)

500g (1 lb) selection of chocolates

150 g (5 oz) chocolate truffles

1.5 metres (5 feet) chocolate-coloured
  ribbon, about 4 cm (1½ inches) wide

1 Put the cake on the plate and spread the ganache over the top
  and sides, smoothing it into an even layer with a palette knife.

2 Unwrap the chocolate bars and gently press a bar against
  each side of the cake so they meet squarely at the corners.

3 Arrange the chocolates and truffles over the top of the cake so
  that they resemble a layer in a box of chocolates. Wrap the
ribbon around the sides of the cake, tying it in a bow.

tip

Use plain or milk chocolate bars for the
sides of the cake but choose thin bars
rather than chunky ones. Remove them
before you cut the cake into portions.

Confetti meringue

serves 8–10
preparation and cooking time about 1½ hours
decoration time 20 minutes

1 Line 2 baking sheets with baking parchment. To make the meringue, whisk the egg whites in a thoroughly cleaned bowl until stiff. Add the sugar, a tablespoonful at a time, whisking well after each addition until the meringue is stiff and glossy.

2 Spread a thin 20 cm (8 inch) circle of meringue on one baking sheet for the base of the cake. Use 2 dessertspoons to place spoonfuls of meringue on baking sheets, spacing them about 3 cm (1¼ inches) apart. (Makes about 28 meringues.) Bake in a preheated oven, 120°C (250°F), Gas Mark ½, for about 1¼ hours until the meringues are crisp, swapping the baking sheets round halfway through cooking. Leave to cool.

3 Mix the cream with the icing sugar and enough rosewater to taste, whipping them together until the mixture is only just holding its shape.

4 Arrange meringues on the serving plate, forming a circle about 20 cm (8 inches) across. Fill in the centre with 2–3 more meringues. Spoon over a little of the cream, then add another layer of meringues. Repeat the layering, building up the meringue into a cone shape and finishing with a single meringue on top.

5 Pull the petals from half the roses and scatter them over the cake. Tuck the whole roses around the base of the meringues. Just before serving, dust generously with the pink sugar.

4 egg whites

225 g (7½ oz) caster sugar

300 ml (½ pint) double cream

1 tablespoon icing sugar

1–2 tablespoons rosewater

flat glass plate, about 25 cm (10 inches) across

6–8 small pink roses

2 tablespoons bought or homemade pink sugar crystals (see tip)

tips

To make the pink sugar, put a little caster sugar in a small bowl and add a tiny dot of pink food colouring paste. Work the paste into the sugar with the back of a teaspoon.

Frosted fruit meringue cake

serves 18
decoration time 45 minutes

3 egg whites

200 g (7 oz) caster sugar

1 fig

several small plums and apricots

10–12 cherries

75 g (3 oz) blueberries

20 cm (8 inch) round bought or homemade
Madeira Cake (see page 11)

single quantity Buttercream (see page 16)

6 tablespoons raspberry or strawberry jam

25 cm (10 inch) round glass plate

2 egg whites

pinch of salt

tips

The meringue must be made and cooked
on the day you serve the cake, but you can
get ahead by baking the cake, sandwiching
it and frosting the fruits a day in advance.

For a special occasion, drizzle the
sponge with lemon or orange liqueur
before spreading it with buttercream.

1 Lightly whisk one egg white in a small bowl until it is broken up. Put half the caster sugar in another bowl. Using your fingers or a large paintbrush coat the fig with egg white, then sprinkle it generously with sugar until it is evenly coated. Transfer it to a sheet of baking parchment. Frost all the remaining fruits and leave them in a cool place for at least 1 hour to dry.

2 Cut the cake horizontally into 3 layers. Sandwich together with the buttercream and jam and place the cake on a baking sheet.

3 Whisk the 2 remaining egg whites with the salt in a thoroughly clean bowl until stiff. Gradually whisk in the remaining caster sugar, a tablespoon at a time, whisking well after each addition until the mixture is smooth and glossy. Use a palette knife to spread a thin layer of the meringue over the top and sides of the cake to seal in any crumbs. Turn the remaining meringue on to the top of the cake and spread it over the cake evenly. Use the tip of the palette knife to mark deep swirls into the meringue.

4 Bake the meringue cake in a preheated oven, 190°C (375°F), Gas Mark 5, for 5–10 minutes until the meringue is toasted. Rotate the baking sheet once or twice during cooking to give an even colour. Take care that the meringue doesn't become too brown.

5 Remove the cake from the oven, transfer to the plate and leave to cool for a few minutes. Arrange the larger fruits on top of the cake, halving some of them if liked. Scatter the cherries and blueberries over the top.

White chocolate frosted cake

serves 12
decoration time 20 minutes

18 cm (7 inch) bought or homemade round
   Madeira Cake (see page 11)

single quantity White Chocolate Ganache
   (see page 18)

25 cm (10 inch) round or square cream-
   coloured platter

8–10 large, cream-coloured, silk flowers
   (see tip)

1 Cut the cake in half horizontally. Sandwich it together with a little of the ganache and place it on the plate.

2 Use a palette knife to spread the remaining ganache over the top and sides of the cake, and finish by swirling it in vertical strokes around the sides.

3 Cut the stems of the flowers down to about 5 cm (2 inches). Alternatively, twist the stems up under each flower so they can be re-shaped and used again. Arrange the flowers over the top of the cake.

tips

The flavours of this simple cake are good enough to enjoy just as they are. However, if you want some extra zing, try using a spicy or an orange- or lemon-flavoured Madeira base or drizzle the sponge with a coffee- or citrus-flavoured liqueur before sandwiching it together.

You can use either very pretty, delicate silk flowers to decorate the cake or more flamboyant ones, as shown opposite. It's really a matter of personal preference.

Index

A

age cakes 118–19
almond paste 23
almonds 74–5
animals
    animal ark 54–5
    man's best friend 56–7
    the one that got away 32–3
    spider's web 98–9

B

baking tins 6, 9
be my Valentine 86–7
birthday cakes
    big birthday 116–17
    birthday present 130–1
    50th birthday 118–19
    happy birthday cupcakes 114–15
boards 21
bonfire night 128–9
bon voyage 40–1
books 38–9
bottle, champagne 132–3
bought cakes 6, 10
box of chocolates 134–5
box of toys 110–11
buttercream 16–17

C

cake boards 21
cake recipes 10–15
cake tins 6, 9
candies 25
candle garland 106–7
champagne bottle 132–3
chocobloc 44–5
chocolate
    box of chocolates 134–5
chocobloc 44–5
chocolate egg cake 90–1
chocolate fudge icing 19
chocolate truffle cake 46–7
chocolate wedding cake 68–9
curls 24
dark chocolate ganache 18
Easter egg 92–3
man's best friend 56–7
melting 25
ribbony chocolate wedding cake 70–1
rich chocolate cake 13
triple chocolate croquembouche 124–5
white chocolate frosted cake 140–1
white chocolate ganache 18
white chocolate wedding cake 66–7
choux pastry buns 15
    triple chocolate croquembouche 124–5
Christmas star 102–3
coloured icing 20–1
confetti meringue 136–7
cupcakes 12
    Easter 94–5
    happy birthday 114–15
    snowy 100–1

D

dark chocolate ganache 18
decorating
    techniques 20–5
    time 6
dogs 56–7

E

Easter
    chocolate egg cake 90–1
    Easter cupcakes 94–5
    Easter egg 92–3
eggs
    chocolate egg cake 90–1
    Easter egg 92–3
engagement 62–3
equipment 6, 8–9

F

feathered hat 48–9
50th birthday 118–19
fillings 16–19
finishing touches 24–5
fireworks night 128–9
first night 58–9
first prize 34–5
fishing 32–3
flavourings 11, 16
flowers
    as decorations 25
    fruit and flowers 76–7
    keeping frosted flowers 88
    layered rose wedding cake 72–3
    vase of flowers 50–1
food colourings 20–1
football boots 28–9
frosted fruit meringue cake 138–9
fruit cake see rich fruit cake
fruit and flowers 76–7

G

ganache 18
gardening
    green fingers 36–7
    pumpkin patch 96–7
garland, candle 106–7
glacé fruit cake 108–9
glittery engagement 62–3
golden wedding cake 82–3
golfer's bag 30–1

graduation cake 38–9
green fingers 36–7

H
happy birthday cupcakes
    114–15
hats 48–9
hearts
    be my Valentine 86–7
    red heart cake 78–9
hiring cake tins 6
home, welcome 42–3

I
icing 16–23
    buttercream 16–17
    chocolate fudge icing 19
    coloured icing 20–1
    covering cake boards 21
    cutting out shapes 24
    ganache 18
    piped 24
    ready-to-roll 20, 22
    royal icing 19
    techniques 20–4
individual cakes
    Easter cupcakes 94–5
    happy birthday cupcakes
        114–15
    snowy cupcakes 100–1

J
jagged jewel cake 104–5

L
layered rose wedding cake 72–3
letters 114–15
lining cake tins 9

M
Madeira cake 11
    big birthday 116–17
    bon voyage 40–1
    Christmas star 102–3
    feathered hat 48–9
    50th birthday 118–19
    fireworks night 128–9
    first night 58–9
    first prize 34–5
    frosted fruit meringue cake 138–9
    glittery engagement 62–3
    golfer's bag 30–1
    graduation cake 38–9
    green fingers 36–7
    happy birthday cupcakes 114–15
    man's best friend 56–7
    Midsummer Night's Dream 126–7
    Mother's Day 88–9
    new parents 52–3
    one that got away, the 32–3
    pumpkin patch 96–7
    red heart cake 78–9
    spider's web 98–9
    summer carnival 122–3
    vase of flowers 50–1
    white chocolate frosted cake 140–1
man's best friend 56–7
melting chocolate 25
meringue
    confetti meringue 136–7
    frosted fruit meringue cake 138–9
metallic colours 20, 32
Midsummer Night's Dream 126–7
Mother's Day 88–9

N
new parents 52–3

O
one that got away, the 32–3

P
painted decorations 25
parents
    Mother's Day 88–9
    new parents 52–3
paste colours 20, 21
piped icing 24
piping bags 24
powder colours 20
preparation in advance 6, 10
pumpkin patch 96–7
purple icing 38

R
ready-made cakes 6, 10
ready-to-roll icing 20, 22
recipes, cake 10–15
red heart cake 78–9
ribbony chocolate wedding cake 70–1
rich chocolate cake 13
    animal ark 54–5
    be my Valentine 86–7
    big birthday 116–17
    box of chocolates 134–5
    chocobloc 44–5
    chocolate egg cake 90–1
    chocolate truffle cake 46–7
    chocolate wedding cake 68–9
    Easter egg 92–3
    man's best friend 56–7
    ribbony chocolate wedding cake 70–1
    summer celebration cake 20–1
    white chocolate wedding cake 66–7
rich fruit cake 14
    birthday present 130–1

box of toys 110–11
candle garland 106–7
fruit and flowers 76–7
glacé fruit cake 108–9
golden wedding cake 82–3
jagged jewel cake 104–5
layered rose wedding cake 72–3
red heart cake 78–9
silver wedding cake 80–1
sugared almond wedding cake 74–5
welcome home 42–3
winter wedding cake 64–5
royal icing 19

S

silver food colouring 32
silver wedding cake 80–1
snowy cupcakes 100–1
spider's web 98–9
sport
    first prize 34–5
    football boots 28–9
    golfer's bag 30–1
    one that got away, the 32–3

stars, Christmas 102–3
sugared almond wedding cake 74–5
suitcases 40–1
summer carnival 122–3
summer celebration cake 120–1
sweets 25
Swiss roll 12
    champagne bottle 132–3
    football boots 28–9

T

theatre 58–9
the one that got away 32–3
time for decoration 6
tins 6, 9
toys, box of 110–11
triple chocolate croquembouche 124–5
trophies 34–5
truffles 46–7

V

Valentine's Day
    be my Valentine 86–7
    red heart cake 78–9

vanilla cupcakes 12
    Easter cupcakes 94–5
    snowy cupcakes 100–1
vase of flowers 50–1

W

wedding cakes
    chocolate wedding cake 68–9
    golden wedding cake 82–3
    layered rose wedding cake 72–3
    red heart cake 78–9
    ribbony chocolate wedding cake 70–1
    silver wedding cake 80–1
    sugared almond wedding cake 74–5
    white chocolate wedding cake 66–7
    winter wedding cake 64–5
welcome home 42–3
white chocolate
    white chocolate frosted cake 140–1
    white chocolate ganache 18
    white chocolate wedding cake 66–7
winter wedding cake 64–5

ACKNOWLEDGEMENTS

Executive Editor Sarah Ford
Editor Charlotte Wilson
Executive Art Editor Karen Sawyer
Designer Jane Forster
Photographer Lis Parsons
Home Economist Joanna Farrow
Production Controller Manjit Sihra
Index Indexing Specialists (UK) Ltd

Hamlyn would like to thank the following for the
supply of equipment and props for phototography:
Paperchase www.paperchase.co.uk
Divertimenti www.divertimenti.co.uk
Muji www.muji.co.uk
The Pier www.thepier.co.uk